MAD FOREST
A Play from Romania

AND

THE SKRIKER

Two Plays by
CARYL CHURCHILL

The Fireside Theatre

NICK HERN BOOKS

CARYL CHURCHILL has written for the stage, television and radio. Her stage plays include *Owners* (Royal Court Threatre Upstairs, 1972); *Objections to Sex and Violence* (Royal Court, 1975); *Light Shining in Buckinghamshire* (Joint Stock on tour, incl. Theatre Upstairs, 1976); *Vinegar Tom* (Monstrous Regiment on tour, incl. Half Moon and ICA, 1976); *Traps* (Threatre Upstairs, 1977), *Cloud Nine* (Joint Stock on tour, incl. Royal Court, London, 1979, then Theatre de Lys, New York, 1981); *Three More Sleepless Nights* (Soho Poly and Theatre Upstairs, 1980); *Top Girls* (Royal Court, London, then Public Theatre, New York, 1982); *Fen* (Joint Stock on tour, incl. Almeida and Royal Court, London, then Public Theatre, New York, 1983); *Softcops* (RSC at the Pit, 1984); *A Mouthful of Birds,* with David Lan (Joint Stock on tour, incl. Royal Court, 1986); *Serious Money* (Royal Court and Wyndham's, London, then Public Theatre, New York, 1987); *Icecream* (Royal Court, London, 1989); *Mad Forest* (Central School of Speech and Drama, then Royal Court, London, 1990, then New York Theatre Workshop, 1991); *Lives of the Great Poisoners* (with Orlando Gough and Ian Spink, Second Stride on tour, incl. Riverside Studios, London, 1991); *The Skriker* (Royal National Theatre, London, 1994); and her translation of Seneca's *Thyestes* (Manchester and Royal Court Theatre, London, 1994).

MAD FOREST

A Play from Romania

CARYL CHURCHILL

Diary of Events

16–17 December

Demonstrations in Timoşoara in support of Hungarian priest Laszlo Tokeş.
Ceauşescu visits Iran. Demonstrators in Timoşoara shot.

21 December

Ceauşescu's speech in Bucharest. He is shouted down. That night shooting.

22 December

Army goes over to people. Ceauşescu escapes. TV station occupied. National Salvation Front formed. More shooting which continues for several days.

25 December

Ceauşescu captured, tried by military tribunal and shot.

Mid-January

Director Mark Wing-Davey suggests Romania project with Central School students to writer Caryl Churchill.

Late January & February

Front announces it will stand in elections. Demonstrations against Front and Iliescu, and in support.

3–7 March

Director and writer go to Romania.

31 March–7 April

Director, writer, designer, lighting designer, 1 stage management and 10 acting students go to Romania, work with students at the Caragiale Institute of Theatre and Cinema, and meet many other people.

May

Anti Front demonstrators block centre of Bucharest.

20 May

Election. Iliescu and Front have large majorities.

21 May

Rehearsals begin.

13 June

Miners enter Bucharest to crush anti-Front demonstrations. First performance of *Mad Forest* at Central School.

17 September

National Theatre, Bucharest. Discussions with audience.

Bucharest Workshop Group

Victoria Alcock, Sarah Ball, Joseph Bennett, Caryl Churchill, Lucy Cohu, Nicola Gibson, Iain Hake, Mark Heal, David Mac-Creedy, Antony McDonald, David Mestecky, Nigel H. Morgan, Indra Ove, Mark Wing-Davey, Jason Woodford.

Bucharest Production Group

Victoria Alcock, Gordon Anderson, Isabel Ashman, Sarah Ball, Joseph Bennett, Caryl Churchill, Lucy Cohu, Nicola Gibson, Iain Gillie, Philip Glenister, Iain Hake, Mark Heal, Rod Langsford, David MacCreedy, Antony McDonald, David Mestecky, Nigel H. Morgan, Jon Morrell, Simon Reynolds, Bianca Schwarz, John Titcombe, Mark Wing-Davey.

Special Thanks to:

The staff and pupils of the Institutul de Arta Teatrala si Cinematografica, I.L.Caragiale, Bucharest; and all the Romanians who helped both groups in Bucharest.

MAD FOREST

On the plain where Bucharest now stands there used to
be 'a large forest crossed by small muddy streams . . . It
could only be crossed on foot and was impenetrable
for the foreigner who did not know the paths . . . The
horsemen of the steppe were compelled to go round it,
and this difficulty, which irked them so, is shown by
the name . . . Teleorman—Mad Forest.'
'A Concise History of Romania', Otetea and MacKenzie

Production Note

Since the play goes from the difficulty of saying anything to everyone talking, don't be afraid of long silences. For instance, in Scene One, the silence before Bogdan turns up the music was a good fifteen seconds in our production. Short scenes like 13 and 15 need to be given their weight. Don't add additional dialogue (for instance in queues, party or arrival in country) except in III 6 where 'etc' means there can be other things shouted by the spectators.

The queue scenes and execution scene should have as many people as are available. In the execution scene it is the violence of the spectators which is the main focus rather than the execution itself.

We didn't use a prop rat.

The Vampire was not dressed as a vampire.

In Part II (December) the language of the different characters varies with how well they speak English, and this should be reflected in their accents.

In the hospital and party scenes it is particularly important that the short scenes within them are not run together and that time has clearly passed.

Music. As in the text, the music after the opening poem becomes the music on the Vladu radio. It's not essential to do what we did with the music, but it may be helpful to know that at the end of the wedding we used a hymn to the Ceauşescus and continued the music till everyone was in place for the beginning of December; at the end of December the whole company sang a verse from 'Wake up Romania' in Romanian, which then merged with a recording of it; we had music at the beginning of Part III. The party music in III 8 should be western euro-pop. The dance music should be the lambada—this is not an arbitrary choice, it was the popular dance at the time. The nightmare scene and the very end of the play probably need sound.

Words for the poem at the beginning and words and music for 'Wake up Romania' can be got from Margaret Ramsay Ltd.

Caryl Churchill and Mark Wing-Davey
March 1991

Mad Forest was first staged by students in their final year of training at the Central School of Speech and Drama, London, on 25 June 1990 with the cast as follows. It was subsequently performed at the National Theatre, Bucharest, from 17 September and opened at the Royal Court Theatre, London on 9 October 1990 with the same cast.

VLADU FAMILY

BOGDAN, an electrician	David MacCreedy
IRINA, a tramdriver	Lucy Cohu
their children:	
LUCIA, a primary school teacher	Nicola Gibson
FLORINA, a nurse	Victoria Alcock
GABRIEL, an engineer	David Mestecky
RODICA, Gabriel's wife	Sarah Ball
WAYNE, Lucia's bridegroom	Gordon Anderson
GRANDFATHER, Bogdan's father	Iain Hake
GRANDMOTHER, Bogdan's mother	Sarah Ball
OLD AUNT, Bogdan's aunt	Iain Hake

ANTONESCU FAMILY

MIHAI, an architect	Gordon Anderson
FLAVIA, a teacher	Sarah Ball
RADU, an art student, their son	Mark Heal
GRANDMOTHER, Flavia's grandmother, who is dead.	Lucy Cohu

IANOŞ	Philip Glenister
SECURITATE MAN	Iain Hake
DOCTOR	Joseph Bennett
PRIEST	Iain Hake
ANGEL	Joseph Bennett
VAMPIRE	Iain Hake
DOG	Gordon Anderson
SOMEONE WITH SORE THROAT	Iain Hake
PATIENT	Joseph Bennett
TWO SOLDIERS	Iain Hake & Joseph Bennett
TOMA, age 8	David MacCreedy

| GHOST | } Joseph Bennett |
| WAITER | |

PAINTER	Philip Glenister
GIRL STUDENT	Lucy Cohu
2 BOY STUDENTS	Joseph Bennett &
	David MacCreedy
TRANSLATOR	Gordon Anderson
BULLDOZER DRIVER	David Mestecky
SECURITATE OFFICER	Mark Heal
SOLDIER	Iain Hake
STUDENT DOCTOR	Nicola Gibson
FLOWERSELLER	Victoria Alcock
HOUSEPAINTER	Sarah Ball

PEOPLE IN QUEUES AND WEDDING GUESTS played by members of the company

Director	Mark Wing-Davey
Designer	Antony McDonald
Lighting Designer	Nigel H. Morgan

Notes on Layout

A speech usually follows the one immediately before it
BUT:

(1) When one character starts speaking before the other has
    finished, the point of interruption is marked / and the first
    character continues talking regardless:

e.g.
GABRIEL: They came to the office yesterday and gave us one
    of their usual pep talks and at the end one of them took me
    aside / and said we'd like to see

IRINA: Wait.
GABRIEL: you tomorrow. So I know what that meant . . .

(2) Sometimes two speakers interrupt at once while the first
    speaker continues:*

e.g.
FLAVIA: Why don't the Front tell the truth and admit they're
    communists? / *Nothing to be

MIHAI: Because they're not.

RADU: *I don't care what they're called, it's the same people.

FLAVIA: ashamed of in communism . . .

Here both MIHAI and RADU interrupt FLAVIA at the same
point.

I LUCIA'S WEDDING

The company recite, smiling, a poem in Romanian in praise of Elena Ceauşescu.

Stirring Romanian music.

Each scene is announced by one of the company reading from a phrasebook as if an English tourist, first in Romanian, then in English, and again in Romanian.

1. Lucia are patru ouă. Lucia has four eggs.

Music continues. Bogdan and Irina Vladu sit in silence, smoking Romanian cigarettes.

Bogdan turns up the music on the radio very loud. He sits looking at Irina.

Irina puts her head close to Bogdan's and talks quickly and quietly, to convince him.

He argues back, she insists, he gets angry. We can't hear anything they say.

They stop talking and sit with the music blaring. Bogdan is about to speak when Florina and Lucia come in, laughing.

They stop laughing and look at Bogdan and Irina.

Irina turns the radio down low.

Lucia produces four eggs with a flourish. Irina kisses her.

Bogdan ignores her.

Lucia produces a packet of American cigarettes.

Florina laughs.

Lucia opens the cigarettes and offers them to Irina. She hesitates, then puts out her cigarette and takes one. Florina takes one.

Bogdan ignores them.

Lucia offers a cigarette to Bogdan, he shakes his head.

Lucia takes a cigarette. They sit smoking.

Bogdan finishes his cigarette. He sits without smoking. Then he takes a cigarette.

Lucia and Florina laugh.

Bogdan picks up an egg and breaks it on the floor.

Irina gathers the other eggs to safety.

Lucia and Florina keep still.

Irina turns the radio up loud and is about to say something.

Bogdan turns the radio completely off. Irina ignores him and smokes.

Florina gets a cup and spoon and scrapes up what she can of the egg off the floor.

Lucia keeps still.

2. Cine are un chibrit? Who has a match?

Antonescu family, noticeably better off than the Vladus. Mihai thinking and making notes, Flavia correcting exercise books, Radu drawing.

They sit in silence for some time. When they talk they don't look up from what they're doing.

MIHAI: He came today.

FLAVIA: That's exciting.

RADU: Did he make you change it?

MIHAI: He had a very interesting recommendation. The arch should be this much higher.

RADU: And the columns?

MIHAI: We will make an improvement to the spacing of the columns.

FLAVIA: That sounds good.

They go on working.

The lights go out. They are resigned, almost indifferent.

Radu takes a match and lights a candle.

They sit in candlelight in silence.

RADU: I don't see why.

FLAVIA: We've said no.

RADU: If I leave it a year or two till after the wedding,
   I / could—

FLAVIA: No.

RADU: It's not her fault if her sister—

MIHAI: The whole family. No. Out of the question.

Pause.

There are plenty of other girls, Radu.

They sit in silence.

The lights come on.

Flavia blows out the candle and snuffs it with her fingers.

They all start reading again.

RADU: So is that the third time he's made you change
   it?

Mihai doesn't reply. They go on working.

3. Ea are o scrisoare din Statele Unite. She has a letter from the United States.

Lucia is reading an airmail letter, smiling. She kisses the letter. She puts it away. Florina comes in from work.

LUCIA: Tired?

Pause. Florina is taking off her shoes.

I'm sorry.

Florina smiles and shrugs.

LUCIA: No but all of you . . . because of me and Wayne.

FLORINA: You love him.

Lucia takes out the letter and offers it to Florina.

Florina hesitates. Lucia insists.

Florina reads the letter, she is serious. Lucia watches her.

Florina gives the letter back.

LUCIA: And Radu? Have you seen him lately?

Florina shrugs.

4. Elevii ascultă lecţia. The pupils listen to the lesson.

Flavia speaks loudly and confidently to her pupils.

FLAVIA: Today we are going to learn about a life dedi-
cated to the happiness of the people and noble ideas of
socialism.

The new history of the motherland is like a great river
with its fundamental starting point in the biography of
our general secretary, the president of the republic,
Comrade Nicolae Ceauşescu, and it flows through the
open spaces of the important dates and problems of
contemporary humanity. Because it's evident to everybody that linked to the personality of this great son of
the nation is everything in the country that is most
durable and harmonious, the huge transformations taking place in all areas of activity, the ever more vigorous
and ascendant path towards the highest stages of progress and civilisation. He is the founder of the country.
More, he is the founder of man. For everything is being
built for the sublime development of man and country,
for their material and spiritual wellbeing. He started
his revolutionary activity in the earliest years of his ad-
olescence in conditions of danger and illegality, there-
fore his life and struggle cannot be detached from the
most burning moments of the people's fight against fas-
cism and war to achieve the ideals of freedom and aspi-
rations of justice and progress.

We will learn the biography under four headings.

1. village of his birth and prison
2. revolution
3. leadership
4. the great personality of Comrade Nicolae Ceauşescu.

5. Cumpărăm carne. We are buying meat.

Radu is in a queue of people with shopping bags. They stand a long time in silence.

Someone leaves a bag with a bottle in it to mark the place and goes. They go on standing.

Radu whispers loudly.

RADU: Down with Ceauşescu.

The woman in front of him starts to look round, then pretends she hasn't heard. The man behind pretends he hasn't heard and casually steps slightly away from Radu.

Two people towards the head of the queue look round and Radu looks round as if wondering who spoke.

They go on queueing.

6. Doi oameni stau la soare. Two men are sitting in the sun.

Bogdan and a Securitate Man.

SECURITATE: Do you love your country?

Bogdan nods.

And how do you show it?

Pause.

You love your country, how do you show it?

Bogdan is about to speak. He stops. He is about to speak.

You encourage your daughter to marry an American.

BOGDAN: No.

SECURITATE: She defies you?

Silence.

Your daughter was trained as a primary school teacher,
she can no longer be employed. Romania has wasted
resources that could have benefited a young woman
with a sense of duty.

Silence.

I understand your wife works as a tramdriver and has
recently been transferred to a depot in the south of the
city which doubles the time she has to travel to work.
You are an electrician, you have been a foreman for
some time but alas no longer. Your son is an engineer
and is so far doing well. Your other daughter is a nurse.
So far there is nothing against her except her sister.

Pause.

I'm sure you are eager to show that your family are
patriots.

Silence. Bogdan looks away.

When they know your daughter wants to marry an
American, people may confide their own shameful
secrets. They may mistakenly think you are someone
who has sympathy with foreign regimes. Your other

children may make undesirable friends who think you're prepared to listen to what they say. They will be right. You will listen.

Pause. Bogdan is about to say something but doesn't.

What?

Pause.

Your colleagues will know you have been demoted and will wrongly suppose that you are short of money. As a patriot you may not have noticed how anyone out of favour attracts the friendship of irresponsible bitter people who feel slighted. Be friendly.

Pause.

What a beautiful day. What a beautiful country.

Silence. Bogdan looks at him.

You will make a report once a week.

7. Ascultaţi? Are you listening?

Lucia and a Doctor.

While they talk the Doctor writes on a piece of paper, pushes it over to Lucia, who writes a reply, and he writes again.

DOCTOR: You're a slut. You've brought this on your-self. The only thing to be said in its favour is that one more child is one more worker.

LUCIA: Yes, I realise that.

DOCTOR: There is no abortion in Romania. I am shocked that you even think of it. I am appalled that you dare suggest I might commit this crime.

LUCIA: Yes, I'm sorry.

Lucia gives the doctor an envelope thick with money and some more money.

DOCTOR: Can you get married?

LUCIA: Yes.

DOCTOR: Good. Get married.

The Doctor writes again, Lucia nods.

DOCTOR: I can do nothing for you. Goodbye.

Lucia smiles. She makes her face serious again.

LUCIA: Goodbye.

8. **Sticla cu vin este pe masă. The bottle of wine is on the table.**

Radu, Gabriel and Ianoş with a bottle of wine. They are in public so they keep their voices down.

IANOŞ: He died and went to heaven and St Peter says, God wants a word with you. So he goes in to see God and God says, 'I hear you think you're greater than me.' And he says, 'Yes, I am.' And God says, 'Right, who made the sun?' 'You did.' 'Who made the stars?' 'You did.' 'Who made the earth?' 'You did.' 'Who made all the people and all the animals and all the trees and all the / plants and—

RADU: And all the wine.

IANOȘ: And everything?' And he said, 'You did, God.' And God says, 'Then how can you possibly be greater than me?' And he says, 'All these things, what did you make them from?' And God said, 'Chaos, I made it all out of Chaos.' 'There you are,' he said, 'I made chaos.'

RADU: A cosmonaut leaves a message for his wife. 'Gone to Mars, back in two weeks.' Two weeks later he comes back and his wife has left him a message. 'Gone shopping, don't know when I'll be back.'

GABRIEL: A man wants a car and he saves up his money and at last he's able to buy a Trabant. He's very proud of it. And he's driving along in his little Trabant and he stops at the traffic lights and bang, a car crashes into the back of it. So he leaps out very angry, and it's a black car with a short numberplate, but he's so angry he doesn't care and he starts banging on the bonnet. Then a big dumper truck stops behind the black car and the driver gets out and he takes a crowbar and he starts smashing the back of the black car. And the Securitate man gets out of his battered black car and he says to the truck driver, 'What's going on? I can understand him being upset because I hit his car, but what's the matter with you?' And the driver says, 'Sorry, I thought it had started.'

9. Cerul este albastru. The sky is blue.

An Angel and a Priest.

ANGEL: Don't be ashamed. When people come into church they are free. Even if they know there are Securitate in church with them. Even if some churches are demolished, so long as there are some churches standing. Even if you say Ceauşescu, Ceauşescu, because the Romanian church is a church of freedom. Not outer freedom of course but inner freedom.

Silence. The Priest sits gazing at the Angel.

PRIEST: This is so sweet, like looking at the colour blue, like looking at the sky when you're a child lying on your back, you stare out at the blue but you're going in, further and further in away from the world, that's. what it's like knowing I can talk to you. Someone says something, you say something back, you're called to a police station, that happened to my brother. So it's not safe to go out to people and when you can't go out sometimes you find you can't go in, I'm afraid to go inside myself, perhaps there's nothing there, I just keep still. But I can talk to you, no one's ever known an angel work for the Securitate, I go out into the blue and I sink down and down inside myself, and yes then I am free inside, I can fly about in that blue, that is what the church can give people, they can fly about inside in that blue.

ANGEL: So when the Romanian church writes a letter to the other Christian churches apologising for not taking a stand / against—

PRIEST: Don't talk about it. I'd just managed to forget.

ANGEL: Don't be ashamed. There was no need for them to write the letter because there's no question of taking a stand, it's not the job of the church / to—

PRIEST: Everyone will think we're cowards.

ANGEL: No no no. Flying about in the blue.

PRIEST: Yes. Yes.

Pause.

You've never been political?

ANGEL: Very little. The Iron Guard used to be rather charming and called themselves the League of the Archangel Michael and carried my picture about. They had lovely processions. So I dabbled.

PRIEST: But they were fascists.

ANGEL: They were mystical.

PRIEST: The Iron Guard threw Jews out of windows in '37, my father remembers it. He shouted and they beat him up.

ANGEL: Politics, you see. Their politics weren't very pleasant. I try to keep clear of the political side. You should do the same.

Pause.

PRIEST: I don't trust you any more.

ANGEL: That's a pity. Who else can you trust?

Pause.

Would you rather feel ashamed?

Pause.

Or are you going to take some kind of action, surely not?

Silence.

PRIEST: Comfort me.

10. Acesta este fratele nostru. This is our brother.

Bogdan, Irina, Lucia, Florina, sitting in the dark with candles. Irina is sewing Lucia's wedding dress.

Gabriel arrives, excited.

GABRIEL: Something happened today. / They came to

IRINA: Wait.

Irina moves to turn on the radio, then remembers it isn't working.

GABRIEL: the office yesterday and gave us their usual pep talk and at the end one of them took me aside / and said we'd like to see you

IRINA: Wait.

GABRIEL: tomorrow. So I knew what that meant, they were going to ask me / to do something for

IRINA: Wait, stop, there's no power.

GABRIEL: them. I prayed all night I'd be strong
enough to say no, I was so afraid I'd be persuaded, /
I've never been brave. So I went in and they said . . .

IRINA: Gaby, stop, be quiet.

FLORINA: No, what if they do hear it, they know what
they did.

GABRIEL: And they said, 'What is patriotism?' I said,
'It's doing all you can, working as hard as possible.'
And they said, / 'We thought you might

BOGDAN: Gabriel.

FLORINA: No, let him.

*Irina puts her hands over her ears. But after a while she
starts to listen again.*

GABRIEL: not understand patriotism because your sister and this and this, but if you're a patriot you'll want
to help us. And I said, 'Of course I'd like to help you,'
and then I actually remembered, listen to this, 'As
Comrade Ceauşescu says, "For each and every citizen
work is an honorary fundamental duty. Each of us
should demonstrate high professional probity, compe-
tence, creativity, devotion and passion in our work."
And because I'm a patriot I work so hard that I can't
think about anything else, I wouldn't be able to listen
to what my colleagues talk about because I have to
concentrate. I work right through the lunch hour.' And
I stuck to it and they couldn't do anything. And I'm so
happy because I've put myself on the other side, I

hardly knew there was one. They made me promise never to tell anyone they'd asked me, and they made me sign something, I didn't care by then, I'd won, so I signed it, not my wife or my parents, it said that specifically because they know what the first thing is you'd do, and of course I'm doing it because I don't care, I'm going straight home to Rodica to tell her, I'm so happy, and I've come to share it with you because I knew you'd be proud of me.

IRINA: But you signed. You shouldn't tell us. I didn't hear.

Florina kisses Gabriel.

FLORINA: But Radu's right to keep away from us.

Pause.

BOGDAN: You're a good boy.

GABRIEL: I was shaking. The first thing when I went in they said—

Bogdan holds up his hand and Gabriel stops.

Pause.

LUCIA: What if I don't get my passport?

11. Uite! Look!

A Soldier and a Waiter stand smoking in the street. Suddenly one of them shouts 'Rat!' and they chase it. Radu, Ianoş and Gabriel pass and join in. The rat is kicked about

like a football. Then Radu, Ianoş and Gabriel go on their
way and the Soldier and the Waiter go back to smoking.

12. Eu o vizitez pe nepoata mea. I am visiting my
    granddaughter.

Flavia and Mihai sitting silently over their work.

Flavia's Grandmother, who is dead. She is an elegant
woman in her 50s.

GRANDMOTHER: Flavia, your life will soon be over.
   You're nearly as old as I was when you were a little girl.
   You thought I was old then but you don't think you're
   old.

FLAVIA: Yes I do. I look at my children's friends and I
   know I'm old.

GRANDMOTHER: No, you still think your life hasn't
   started. You think it's ahead.

FLAVIA: Everyone feels like that.

GRANDMOTHER: How do you know? Who do you
   talk to? Your closest friend is your grandmother and
   I'm dead, Flavia, don't forget that or you really will be
   mad.

FLAVIA: You want me to live in the past? I do, I remember being six years old in the mountains, isn't that
   what old people do?

GRANDMOTHER: You remember being a child,

Flavia, because you're childish. You remember expecting a treat.

FLAVIA: Isn't that good? Imagine still having hope at my age. I admire myself.

GRANDMOTHER: You're pretending this isn't your life. You think it's going to happen some other time. When you're dead you'll realise you were alive now. When I was your age the war was starting. I welcomed the Nazis because I thought they'd protect us from the Russians and I welcomed the Communists because I thought they'd protect us from the Germans. I had no principles. My husband was killed. But at least I knew that was what happened to me. There were things I did. I did them. Or sometimes I did nothing. It was me doing nothing.

Silence.

FLAVIA: Mihai.

MIHAI: Mm?

FLAVIA: Do you ever think . . . if you think of something you'll do . . . do you ever think you'll be young when you do it? Do you think I'll do that next time I'm twenty? Not really exactly think it because of course it doesn't make sense but almost . . . not exactly think it but . . .

Mihai shakes his head and goes back to his work.

FLAVIA: Yes, my life is over.

GRANDMOTHER: I didn't say that.

FLAVIA: I don't envy the young, there's nothing ahead
for them either. I'm nearer dying and that's fine.

GRANDMOTHER: You're not used to listening. What
did I say?

Pause.

FLAVIA: But nobody's living. You can't blame me.

GRANDMOTHER: You'd better start.

FLAVIA: No, Granny, it would hurt.

GRANDMOTHER: Well.

Silence.

FLAVIA: Mihai.

Mihai goes on working.

Mihai.

He looks up.

Silence.

13. Ce oră este? What's the time?

*Lucia and Ianoş standing in silence with their arms round
each other.*

She looks at her watch, he puts his hand over it.

They go on standing.

14. Unde este troleibuzul? Where is the trolleybus?

People waiting for a bus, including Radu.

Florina joins the queue. She doesn't see him.

He sees her. He looks away.

She sees him without him noticing, she looks away.

He looks at her again, they see each other and greet each other awkwardly. They look away.

Radu goes up to her.

RADU: How are you?

FLORINA: Fine.

RADU: And your family?

FLORINA: Fine, and yours?

RADU: So when's Lucia's wedding?

FLORINA: You know when it is.

They stand apart waiting for the bus.

15. Pe Irina o doare capul. Irina has a headache.

Lucia is trying on her wedding dress, helped by Irina.

16. Lucia are o coroană de aur. Lucia has a golden crown.

The wedding. Lucia and Wayne are being married by the Priest. Bogdan, Irina, Florina, Gabriel and Rodica. Other guests.

Two wedding crowns. The Priest crosses Wayne with a crown, saying:

PRIEST: The servant of God Wayne is crowned for the handmaid of God Lucia, in the name of the father, and of the son, and of the holy spirit.

ALL (*sing*):   Amen.

This is repeated three times, then the Priest puts the crown on Wayne's head. He crosses Lucia with a crown saying

PRIEST: The handmaid of God Lucia is crowned for the servant of God Wayne, in the name of the father, and of the son, and of the holy spirit.

ALL (*sing*):   Amen.

This is repeated three times, then the Priest puts the crown on Lucia's head.

Music.

II DECEMBER

None of the characters in this section are the characters in the play that began in part I. They are all Romanians speaking to us in English with Romanian accents. Each behaves as if the others are not there and each is the only one telling what happened.

PAINTER: My name is Valentin Bărbat, I am a painter, I hope to go to the Art Institute. I like to paint horses. Other things too but I like horses. On December 20 my girlfriend got a call, go to the Palace Square. People were wearing black armbands for Timişoara. There was plenty of people but no courage. Nothing happened that day and we went home.

GIRL STUDENT: My name's Natalia Moraru, I'm a student. On the 21st of December I had a row with my mother at breakfast about something trivial and I went out in a rage. There was nothing unusual, some old men talking, a few plainclothes policemen, they think they're clever but everyone knows who they are because of their squashed faces.

TRANSLATOR: I'm Dimitru Constantinescu, I work as a translator in a translation agency. On the 21st we were listening to the radio in the office to hear Ceauşescu's speech. It was frightfully predictable. People had been brought from factories and institutes on buses and he wanted their approval for putting down what he called the hooligans in Timişoara. Then suddenly we heard boos and the radio went dead. So we knew something had happened. We were awfully startled. Everyone was shaking.

BOY STUDENT 1:   My name is Cornel Drăgan, I am a student and I watch the speech on TV. The TV went dead, I was sure at last something happens so I go out to see.

GIRL STUDENT: I went into a shop and heard something had been organised by Ceauşescu and the roads were blocked by traffic. I thought I'd walk to the People's Palace.

BULLDOZER DRIVER: My name is Ilie Barbu. I can work many machines. I work in all the country to build hospitals and schools. Always build, never pull down. In December I work at the People's Palace, I drive a bulldozer. There are always many Securitate and today they make us scared because they are scared.

BOY STUDENT 1:   I see people running away and I try to stop them to ask what is happening but nobody has courage to talk. At last someone says, Let's hope it has started.

BOY STUDENT 2:   Well, I'm Stefan Rusu, in fact I come from Craiova, I only live in Bucharest since September to study. On the 21 no one in our zone knew what was going on. My uncle had just come back from Iran so my sister and I went to meet him and my mother. In the Callea Vittoria I saw Securitate who were upset, they were whispering. Well in fact Securitate have come to me when I was working and asked me to write reports on my colleagues. I agreed because I would get a passport and go to America, but I never wrote anything bad to get someone in trouble. Nobody knew I did this with Securitate. Now I could see the Securitate in the street were scared. Cars were breaking the rules and driving the wrong way up the road. We went to the Intercontinental Hotel but we were not allowed to have a meal. We were whispering, my mother told us she had been in the square and heard people booing.

STUDENT 1:   I got to the square and people are shouting against Ceauşescu, shouting 'Today in Timişoara, tomorrow in all the country.' I look at their lips to believe they say it. I see a friend and at first I don't know him, his face has changed, and when he looks at me I know my face is changed also.

DOCTOR: My name is Ileana Chiriţa. I'm a student doctor, I come to this hospital from school, we must get six months' practical. The 21 was a normal day on duty, I didn't know anything.

GIRL STUDENT: On my way to the People's Palace I saw people queueing for a new thriller that had just been published, so as I was feeling guilty about my mother I decided to try and buy one, thrillers are her favourite books. So I queued to get the book, and at about one o'clock I went home.

BULLDOZER DRIVER: I leave work to get my son from school and I don't go back to work, I go to the Palace Square.

STUDENT 1:   There were two camps, army and people, but nobody shooting. Some workers from the People's Palace come with construction material to make barricades. More and more people come, we are pushed together.

DOCTOR: On my way home in the afternoon there was a woman crying because she lost her handbag, the other women comfort her saying, 'It could be worse, people were crushed and lost their shoes, don't cry for such a small thing.'

SECURITATE: Claudiu Brad, I am an officer in Securitate. In everything I did I think I was right, including the 21. I went to military high school because I like uniforms. My family has no money for me to study but I did well. I went to the Officers School of Securitate and got in the external department, which is best, the worst ones go in the fire service. Nobody knows I am in Securitate except one friend I have since I am three years old. I have no other friends but I like women and recruit them sometimes with clothes. On December 21 I am taking the pulse of the street in plain clothes with a walkie-talkie hidden. My district is Rossetti Place. I report every three hours if the crowd move their position, how could they be made calm, what they want.

SOLDIER: My name is Gheorghe Marin. I am in the army from September. My mother is in house, my father mechanic in railway. December I am near the airport. They say Hungarians come from Hungary into Romania, we must shoot them. They give us four magazines. Before, we work in the fields, we have one lessons to shoot. 21 we are in trenches, we have spades to dig. We wait something, we don't know what. We don't know Ceauşescu speak, we don't know what happen in Bucharest.

GIRL STUDENT: I'd planned to go to see a film with a

friend but in the afternoon my father said I must ring up and pretend to be ill, then my friend rang and said that she is ill. I wanted to go out and my father said I couldn't go alone. I thought of an excuse—we had to have some bread, so we went out together. There were a lot of people moving from Union Place towards University Place and I heard someone shout, 'Down with the Dictator.' I was very confused. This was opposed to the policy of the leading forces. A man came up and asked what was happening but my father pulled me away because he realised the man was a provoker who starts arguments and then reports the people who get involved. My father insisted we go home, I said he was a coward and began to cry. He said if he was single he would behave differently.

BULLDOZER DRIVER: In the square there is much army and tanks. My son is six years old, I am scared for him. I take him home and we watch what happens on TV with my wife and daughter.

STUDENT 2:   About five o'clock we heard people shouting 'Jos Ceauşescu.' My uncle wanted to go home to Cluj. Walking back I noticed it was 99% young people in the square with police and soldiers near them and I thought 'That's the end for them.' At home we tried to avoid the topic and get it out of our minds.

STUDENT 1:   There are vans bringing drink and I tell people not to drink because Securitate wants to get us drunk so we look bad. In the evening we tried to make a barricade in Rosetti Place. We set fire to a truck.

SECURITATE: There are barricades and cars burning in my district, I report it. Later the army shoot the people and drive tanks in them. I go off duty.

HOUSEPAINTER: My name is Margareta Antoniu, my work is a housepainter. I paint the windows on the big apartment blocks. I come back to work just now because I have a baby. The 21, the evening, I come home from a village with my children and my husband says it is happening. We expect it because of Timişoara. He hear tanks and shooting like an earthquake. We are happy someone fight for our people.

DOCTOR: My husband was away to visit his parents and I felt lonely. My mother phoned and warned me to stay home and said, 'Listen to the cassette'—this is our code for Radio Free Europe.

FLOWERSELLER: My name is Cornelia Dediliuc. I am a flowerseller, 22 years. Three children, 7, 4 and 2. I have a great pain because my mother die three weeks. My husband is very good, we meet when I am 14, before him I know only school and home. Before I tell you December I tell you something before in my family. My son who is 4 is 2, we live in a small room, I cook, I go out and my child pull off the hot water and hurt very bad. I come in and see, I have my big child 5 my hands on his neck because he not take care. Now I have illness, I have headache, and sometimes I don't know what I do. When the revolution start I am home with my children. The shooting is very big. I hold my children and stay there.

PAINTER: When we heard shooting we went out, and we stayed near the Intercontinental Hotel till nearly midnight. I had an empty soul. I didn't know who I was.

STUDENT 1: They shot tracer bullets with the real bullets to show they were shooting high. At first people

don't believe they will shoot in the crowd again after
Timişoara.

PAINTER: I saw a tank drive into the crowd, a man's
head was crushed. When people were killed like that
more people came in front of the tanks.

FLOWERSELLER: My husband come home scared,
he has seen dead people. I say him please not to go out
again because the children.

GIRL STUDENT: At about 11 my family began to ar-
gue so I went to my room. I heard shooting and called
my father. He wouldn't let me open the shutter but
through the crack I saw a wounded army officer running across the street screaming.

PAINTER: It's enough to see one person dead to get
empty of feeling.

FLOWERSELLER: But I sleep and he goes out. I can't
see something because the window of the apartment is
not that way but I hear the shooting.

STUDENT 2: My mother, sister and I all slept in the
same room that night because we were scared.

DOCTOR: The block of flats was very quiet. Lights
were on very late. I could hear other people listening
to the radio.

GIRL STUDENT: I sat up till four in the morning. I
wanted to go out but my father had locked the door and
hidden the key.

STUDENT 1: At four in the morning I telephone my mother and tell her peoples are being killed.

PAINTER: That night it seems it must be all over. I hope it will go on tomorrow but don't know how.

SECURITATE: In the night the army cleaned the blood off the streets and painted the walls and put tar on the ground where there were stains from the blood so everything was clean.

STUDENT 1: At six in the morning there is new tar on the road but I see blood and something that is a piece of skin. Someone puts down a white cloth on the blood and peoples throw money, flowers, candles, that is the beginning of the shrines.

DOCTOR: On my way to work on the morning of the 22 there were broken windows and people washing the street.

BULLDOZER DRIVER: On the 22 I go back to work. I am afraid I am in trouble with Securitate because I leave work the day before but nobody says nothing.

DOCTOR: At the hospital no one knew what had happened but there were 14 dead and 19 wounded. There were two kinds of wounds, normal bullet wounds and bullets that explode when they strike something and break bones in little pieces, there is no way of repairing them.

HOUSEPAINTER: About 7 o'clock I take a shower. I hear a noise in the street. I look out, I see thousands of workers from the Industrial Platforms. I am wet, I have

no clothes, I stay to watch. They are more and more,
two three kilometres. Now I know Ceauşescu is finish.

DOCTOR: At about 8 I saw out of the window people
going towards University Square holding flags. They
pass a church and suddenly they all knelt down in silence. My colleagues began to say, He will fall. An old
doctor, 64 years old, climbed to a dangerous place to
get down Ceauşescu's picture and we all cheered. We
heard on the radio the General in charge of the Army
had killed himself and been announced a traitor. We
kept treating patients and running back to the radio.

STUDENT 2:   We heard that the General committed
suicide and there was a state of emergency declared. I
thought everything is lost.

GIRL STUDENT: I insisted we go out. My father
dressed like a bride taking a long time.

FLOWERSELLER: I go to the market to get food and
many people are going to the centre. I watch them go
by. I am sorry I get married so young.

TRANSLATOR: I went to work as usual but there was
only one colleague in my office. We heard shots so we
went out. I've noticed in films people scatter away from
gunfire but here people came out saying, What's that?
People were shouting, 'Come with us,' so we went in
the courtyard and shouted too.

GIRL STUDENT: We hadn't gone far when we saw a
crowd of people with banners with Jos Ceauşescu,
shouting, 'Come and join us.' They were low class men
so we didn't know if we could trust them. I suggested

we cross the road so no one could say we were with them.

TRANSLATOR: I heard people shouting, 'Down with Ceaușescu,' for the first time. It was a wonderful feeling to say those words, Jos Ceaușescu.

GIRL STUDENT: Suddenly there was a huge crowd with young people. For the first time I saw the flag with the hole cut out of it. I began to cry, I felt ashamed I hadn't done anything. My father agreed to go on but not with the crowd.

STUDENT 2: Then I saw students singing with flags with holes in them and I thought, Surely this is the end. I walked on the pavement beside them, quickly looking to the side for an escape route like a wild animal.

TRANSLATOR: I had promised my wife to take care. We were walking towards the tanks and I was in a funk. But when you're with other people you keep walking on.

GIRL STUDENT: We came to University Place. For the first time I saw blood, it was smeared on a wooden cross. It's one thing to hear shooting but another to see blood. There were police in front of the Intercontinental Hotel. But in a crowd you disappear and feel stronger.

TRANSLATOR: Then I saw there were flowers in the guns.

GIRL STUDENT: I saw a tank with a soldier holding a red carnation.

TRANSLATOR: Everyone was hugging and kissing each other, you were kissing a chap you'd never seen before.

GIRL STUDENT: And when I looked again the police had vanished.

STUDENT 2: I saw people climbing on army vehicles, I thought they'd taken them from the soldiers, then I realised the soldiers were driving and I heard people shouting, 'The army is with us.' Then I started to cry and I shouted too, 'The army is with us.'

TRANSLATOR: There were no words in Romanian or English for how happy I was.

SECURITATE: On the 22 the army went over to the side of the people. I gave my pistol to an army officer and both magazines were full. That's why I'm here now. I had no more superiors and I wanted to get home. I caught the train and stayed in watching what happened on TV.

HOUSEPAINTER: We leave our six children with my mother and we follow some tanks with people on them. They are go to the TV station. We are there with the first people who make revolution.

BULLDOZER DRIVER: I work till half past ten or eleven, then I see tanks not with army, with men on them. I think I will take the bulldozer. But when I get to the gates my boss says, 'There is no need, Ceauşescu is no more, Ceauşescu nu mai e.' I see no Securitate so I go home to my family.

DOCTOR: Out of the window I saw a silver helicopter

and pieces of paper falling—we thought the people had won and they were celebration papers.

GIRL STUDENT: There were leaflets thrown down from helicopters saying, Go home and spend Christmas with your family.

DOCTOR: A boo went up outside when people saw what they said.

GIRL STUDENT: Suddenly I heard bangbang and I thought my heart would explode, but it was small children throwing celebration crackers against the walls. My father had an attack of cramp and couldn't move any further.

STUDENT 1: In the Palace Square when the tanks turn round we are afraid they will fire on us again. But they turn towards Ceauşescu's balcony.

STUDENT 2: I saw books and papers thrown down from the balcony and I thought I must do something so I went to the radio station. I heard people singing 'Wake Up Romanian' and realised it was a victory.

DOCTOR: About 12.30 I heard on the radio 'Wake Up Romanian,' the anthem which used to be banned, and announcers who apologise for not telling the truth, they had been made to lie. Everyone began to cry and laugh. The doctors and the orderlies were equal.

GIRL STUDENT: We saw an appeal on TV at a friend's house for blood so I went to the hospital with our friend's son-in-law. There were hundreds of people waiting to give blood but only fifty bottles, luckily I was able to give blood.

STUDENT 2: I bought some champagne and went home to my family to celebrate.

DOCTOR: I went home about 3 and my husband has bought 6 bottles of champagne and we called our neighbours in. For the first time in my life I felt free to laugh.

GIRL STUDENT: We went to the TV station, it was surrounded by cars beeping, soldiers wearing arm-bands to show they were with the people. We were told the water was poisoned by Securitate so I ran to buy some milk so my doggie could have something to drink.

STUDENT 1: In the afternoon I go to meet my mother when she comes out of the school. Everyone is shouting Ole ole ole ole and cars hoot their horns. Then I go to see my grandmother to show her I am all right.

Pause.

PAINTER: That night the terror shooting started. There was no quiet place.

TRANSLATOR: When the terror shooting started, I was at home and heard it. My legs buckled, I vomited, I couldn't go out. It took me weeks to get over that.

STUDENT 1: About 7 o'clock we heard on the radio, 'Help, our building is being attacked.' So I went out again.

HOUSEPAINTER: At the radio station I am scared, my husband says, 'Why you come then?' Terroristi shoot from a building and my husband goes with men inside

and catch them. There are many wounded and I help. I
am the only woman.

SOLDIER: They say us it is not Hungarians. It is terroristi. We guard the airport. We shoots anything, we
shoots our friend. I want to stay alive.

PAINTER: They are asking on TV for people to defend
the TV station. My girlfriend and I go out. We stop a
truck of young people and ask where they're going,
they say, 'We are going to die.' They say it like that. We
can do nothing there, everyone knows it.

STUDENT 1:   There was a gypsy who had a gun and he
says, 'Come with me, I want people strong with courage.' He says we must go to the factory of August 23
where they have guns for the guards. The Romanian
people are cowards and have no courage to get in the
truck, but at last we go to the factory. There are more
than one hundred people but only 28 get guns, I get
one, they say, 'Be careful and come back with the gun.'
Then we go to a police station because we know they
are on the side of the people and we ask for bullets. At
first they don't want to give them, they say, 'We need
them to defend our building.' We say, 'Give us at least
one bullet each to be of some use.'

STUDENT 2:   People were shouting, 'Come with us,'
but I thought, 'It's a romantic action, it's useless to go
and fight and die.' I thought I was a coward to be
scared. But I thought, 'I will die like a fool protecting
someone I don't know. How can I stop bullets with my
bare hands? It's the job of the army, I can do nothing, I
will just die.' So I went home.

BOY STUDENT 1:   At the TV station I am behind the

wall of a house and they shoot across me from both
sides. I go into a house, the terroristi are gone, I telephone my mother to tell her where I am. If I stay ten
minutes longer I am dead because they shoot that
house. In the road a boy stands up and is shot. A month
later is his eighteenth birthday. I ask myself if he is
shot by our soldiers. I am standing looking round, bullets are flying. After a while you don't feel scared.

PAINTER: My girlfriend and I were at the TV station. I
didn't know who we were fighting with or how bad it
was. I was just acting to save our lives. It is terrible to
hate and not to be able to do something real.

GIRL STUDENT: That evening I wanted to put on my
army clothes and go out and shoot—I got three out of
three in the shooting test when I was in the army. But
my father had locked the door again and hidden the
key.

HOUSEPAINTER: At ten o'clock we go back to the TV
station with some bread.

STUDENT 1:   A lot of people bring tea and food though
they didn't know if there will be better days and more
to eat. They bring things they save for Christmas. Some
people say the food is poisoned so that people who
bring it must eat and drink first.

PAINTER: I was with my girlfriend so I felt I should
act as a man and be confident. I was curious to know
what I would feel in difficult moments.

STUDENT 1:   There are children of 12 or 13 moving
everywhere, they are harder to see, bringing us bullets,
saying, 'What do you need? What shall I bring you?'

PAINTER: A man was shot in the throat in front of me. Some people couldn't look but I was staring, trying not to forget. I had an insane curiosity. It was like an abattoir. He was like an animal dying with no chance. He had an expression of confusedness. It was incredible he had so much blood. I felt empty.

HOUSEPAINTER: At halfpast eight we go to buy some bread, then home to sleep. My mother ask where I was and I say I go out to buy some bread, just that.

DOCTOR: On the 23 I went to work. Two boys came in with a young man on a stretcher, which they put down, then one of them fell to the ground and began to scream—he sees the wounded man is his older brother. His friend takes him down the hall to get a tranquilliser, it is very dark and when they come back the friend trips over something, it is the body of the older brother, who is dead waiting for surgery. The younger brother was only 14. He threw himself on the corpse and won't move, he said he wants to die with his brother.

STUDENT 1: On the morning of the 23 I went home and I slept for two hours. I kept the gun with me in bed.

GIRL STUDENT: I was about to go out to defend my school when my grandmother began to panic and we thought she would have a heart attack, so I promised to stay in, and I spent the day passing messages to people on the phone. Some people don't like me because of my father.

STUDENT 2: The train didn't go that day so I stayed at

home. I thought, 'This is not my town. I will go to my
own town and act there.'

DOCTOR: I stayed in the hospital without going home
till the 28. We had enough medicine for immediate
cases. Once or twice we had to use out of date anaes-
thetic and the patient woke up during the operation,
not often but it happened. We had no coffee or food.
When my husband came to see me, more than seeing
him I was pleased he had 30 packets of cigarettes. We
ate what the patients left and people brought some
bread and some jam so on Christmas day we had jam
sandwiches.

SECURITATE: When I heard about the execution on
the 25 I came at night with my father to the authorities
to certify what I was doing during the event. I was
detained three days by the army, then told to remain at
home. I will say one thing. Until noon on the 22 we
were law and order. We were brought up in this idea. I
will never agree with unorder. Everyone looks at me
like I did something wrong. It was the way the law was
then and the way they all accepted it.

STUDENT 1: On the 25 we hear about the trial and
their deaths. It is announced that people must return
their weapons so we go to the factory and give back our
guns. Of the 28 who had guns only 4 are alive.

BULLDOZER DRIVER: I stay home with my family
till the 28, then I go to work. They say the time I was

home will be off my holidays. There is no more work on the People's Palace, nobody knows if they finish it.

PAINTER: Painting doesn't mean just describing, it's a state of spirit. I didn't want to paint for a long time then.

III   FLORINA'S WEDDING

1. Cîinelui îi e foame. The dog is hungry.

Night, outside. A shrine. A Dog is lying asleep. A man approaches. He whistles. The Dog looks up. The man whistles. The Dog gets up and approaches, undecided between eagerness and fear. The man is a Vampire.

VAMPIRE: Good dog. Don't be frightened.

Dog approaches, then stops. Growls. Retreats, advances. Growls.

No no no no no. You can tell of course. Yes, I'm not a human being, what does that matter? It means you can talk to me.

DOG: Are you dead?

VAMPIRE: No, no I'm not unfortunately. I'm undead and getting tired of it. I'm a vampire, you may not have met one before, I usually live in the mountains and you look like a dog who's lived on scraps in the city. How old are you?

DOG: Five, six.

VAMPIRE: You look older but that's starvation. I'm

over five hundred but I look younger, I don't go hungry.

DOG: Do you eat dogs?

VAMPIRE: Don't be frightened of me, I'm not hungry now. And if I was all I'd do is sip a little of your blood, I don't eat. I don't care for dogs' blood.

DOG: People's blood?

VAMPIRE: I came here for the revolution, I could smell it a long way off.

DOG: I've tasted man's blood. It was thick on the road, I gobbled it up quick, then somebody kicked me.

VAMPIRE: Nobody knew who was doing the killing, I could come up behind a man in a crowd.

DOG: Good times.

VAMPIRE: There's been a lot of good times over the years.

DOG: Not for me.

VAMPIRE: Do you belong to anyone?

DOG: I used to but he threw me out. I miss him. I hate him.

VAMPIRE: He probably couldn't feed you.

DOG: He beat me. But now nobody talks to me.

VAMPIRE: I'm talking to you.

DOG: Will you keep me?

VAMPIRE: No, I'm just passing the time.

DOG: Please. I'm nice. I'm hungry.

VAMPIRE: Vampires don't keep pets.

DOG: You could feed me.

Dog approaches Vampire carefully.

VAMPIRE: I've no money to buy food for you, I don't buy food, I put my mouth to a neck in the night, it's a solitary—get off.

As the Dog reaches him he makes a violent gesture and the Dog leaps away.

DOG: Don't throw stones at me, I hate it when they throw stones, I hate being kicked, please please I'd be a good dog, I'd bite your enemies. Don't hurt me.

VAMPIRE: I'm not hurting you. Don't get hysterical.

Dog approaches again.

DOG: I'm hungry. You're kind. I'm your dog.

Dog is licking his hands.

VAMPIRE: Stop it, go away. Go. Go. Go away.

Dog slinks a little further off then approaches carefully.

DOG: I'm your dog. Nice. Yes? Your dog? Yes?

VAMPIRE: You want me to make you into a vampire? A vampire dog?

DOG: Yes please, yes yes.

VAMPIRE: It means sleeping all day and going about at night.

DOG: I'd like that.

VAMPIRE: Going about looking like anyone else, being friendly, nobody knowing you.

DOG: I'd like that.

VAMPIRE: Living forever, / you've no idea. All that

DOG: I'd—

VAMPIRE: happens is you begin to want blood, you try to put it off, you're bored with killing, but you can't sit quiet, you can't settle to anything, your limbs ache, your head burns, you have to keep moving faster and faster, that eases the pain, seeking. And finding. Ah.

DOG: I'd like that.

VAMPIRE: And then it's over and you wander round looking for someone to talk to. That's all. Every night. Over and over.

DOG: You could talk to me. I could talk to you. I'm your dog.

VAMPIRE: Yes, if you like, I don't mind. Come here.
   Good dog.

Vampire puts his mouth to the Dog's neck.

**2. Toată lumea speră ca Gabriel să se însănătoşească
repede. Everyone hopes Gabriel will feel better soon.**

i.

Gabriel is in bed in hospital.

Florina, working there as a nurse, passes his bed.

FLORINA: I see less of you working here than if I
   came for a visit.

GABRIEL: Wait.

FLORINA: I can't.

GABRIEL: We won. Eh? Ole . . . Yes?

FLORINA: Yes but don't talk. Wait for your visitors.

GABRIEL: Rodica?

FLORINA: Mum and dad.

GABRIEL: Something wrong with Rodica?

FLORINA: No.

GABRIEL: You'd tell me / if she was hurt.

FLORINA: Don't talk, Gabriel, rest. She's not hurt.

GABRIEL: Do nurses tell the truth?

FLORINA: I do to you.

She goes.

Irina and Bogdan arrive with food.

IRINA: Eggs in the shops. We're getting the benefit already. I'll ask Florina who I should give it to. Keep the apples here. Make sure you get it all, you fought for it.

GABRIEL: Where's Rodica?

IRINA: She couldn't come.

GABRIEL: I want her.

IRINA: Don't, don't, you're not well, I'll never forgive her, she's perfectly all right.

GABRIEL: What?

IRINA: She's frightened to go out. Now when there's nothing happening. She sends her love.

Bogdan has a bottle of whisky.

BOGDAN: This is for the doctor. / Which doctor

GABRIEL: No need.

BOGDAN: do I give it to?

GABRIEL: No.

IRINA: Yes, a little present for the doctor so he's gentle with you.

GABRIEL: That was before. Not now.

BOGDAN: When your mother had her operation, two bottles of whisky and then it was the wrong doctor.

IRINA: They can't change things so quickly, Gaby.

BOGDAN: You do something for somebody, he does something for you. Won't change that. Give my father a cigarette, he puts it behind his ear. Because you never know.

GABRIEL: Different now.

BOGDAN: Who shall I give it to? I'll ask Florina.

Mihai, Flavia and Radu arrive. Radu takes Gabriel's hand.

MIHAI: Radu wanted to visit his friend Gabriel so we thought we'd come with him.

FLAVIA: We've brought a few little things.

MIHAI: To pay our respects to a hero.

They stand awkwardly. Then Flavia embraces Irina.

IRINA: Radu's a hero too.

FLAVIA: The young show us the way.

BOGDAN: We're glad you're safe, Radu.

FLAVIA: And Florina's here?

IRINA: Yes, she's working.

MIHAI: You must be proud of her.

BOGDAN: She worked for five days without stopping.

RADU: I'll go and find her.

FLAVIA: Yes, find her, Radu.

Radu goes.

MIHAI: We're so glad the young people no longer have a misunderstanding. We have to put the past behind us and go forward on a new basis.

BOGDAN: Yes, nobody can be blamed for what happened in the past.

IRINA: Are you warm enough, Gaby? I can bring a blanket from home.

ii.

Evening in the hospital. Patient(s) in dressing-gown(s). Someone comes looking for a doctor.

SORE THROAT: I'm looking for the doctor. I have a sore throat. I need to get an antibiotic.

A patient shuffles slowly about, taking the person down corridors and opening doors, looking for a doctor. Different sounds come from the rooms—a woman crying, a man muttering (it's the patient from iii, we barely hear what

he's saying, just get the sound of constant questions), a
priest chanting. They go off, still looking.

iii.

A couple of weeks after i. Sunlight. Gabriel is much better,
sitting up. Rodica is sitting beside him holding his hand.
Flowers. A Patient in a dressing-gown comes to talk to
them.

PATIENT: Did we have a revolution or a putsch? Who
was shooting on the 21st? And who was shooting on the
22nd? Was the army shooting on the 21st or did some
shoot and some not shoot or were the Securitate dis-
guised in army uniforms? If the army were shooting,
why haven't they been brought to justice? And were
they still shooting on the 22nd? Were they now dis-
guised as Securitate? Most important of all, were the
terrorists and the army really fighting or were they only
pretending to fight? And for whose benefit? And by
whose orders? Where did the flags come from? Who
put loudhailers in the square? How could they publish
a newspaper so soon? Why did no one turn off the
power at the TV? Who got Ceauşescu to call everyone
together? And is he really dead? How many people
died at Timişoara? And where are the bodies? Who
mutilated the bodies? And were they mutilated after
they'd been killed specially to provoke a revolution? By
whom? For whose benefit? Or was there a drug in the
food and water at Timişoara to make people more aggressive? Who poisoned the water in Bucharest?

GABRIEL: Please stop.

PATIENT: Why weren't we shown the film of the execution?

GABRIEL: He is dead.

PATIENT: And is the water still poisoned?

GABRIEL: No.

PATIENT: And who was shooting on the 22nd?

GABRIEL: The army, which was on the side of the people, was fighting the terrorists, who were supporting Ceauşescu.

PATIENT: They changed clothes.

GABRIEL: Who changed clothes?

PATIENT: It was a fancy dress party. Weren't you there? Didn't you see them singing and dancing?

GABRIEL: My sister's coming from America.

PATIENT: Does she know what happened?

GABRIEL: She'll have read the newspapers.

PATIENT: Then you must tell her. Do you know?

GABRIEL: I can't talk about it now.

PATIENT: Are you a Communist?

GABRIEL: No but my sister's / coming now.

PATIENT: Communist. I hope you die.

Florina, Radu and Lucia.

Lucia embraces Gabriel and Rodica.

LUCIA: All the way over on the plane I was terrified of
what I was going to see. But you look beautiful. In
America everyone's thrilled. I told my friends, 'My
brother was there, he was wounded, he's a hero.' I
watched TV but they never showed enough, I kept
playing it and stopping when there was a crowd, I
thought I must know somebody, I was crying all the
time, I was so ashamed not to be here. I've brought you
some chocolate, and oranges.

GABRIEL: How's America?

LUCIA: If you mean how's Wayne he's fine, he has an
allergy but let's forget that, he has a lot of meetings so
he can't be here. But America. There are walls of fruit
in America, five different kinds of apples, and oranges,
grapes, pears, bananas, melons, different kinds of
melon, and things I don't know the name—and the
vegetables, the aubergines are a purple they look as if
they've been varnished, red yellow green peppers,
white onions red onions, bright orange carrots somebody has shone every carrot, and the greens, cabbage
spinach broad beans courgettes, I still stare every time
I go shopping. And the garbage, everyone throws away
great bags full of food and paper and tins, every day,
huge bags, huge dustbins, people live out of them. Eat
some chocolate.

They eat the chocolate.

Patient comes back again.

PATIENT: Have they told you who was shooting on the
22nd? / And why was it necessary to kill

GABRIEL: Please, not now.

PATIENT: Ceauşescu so quickly?

LUCIA: Have some chocolate.

Patient takes some chocolate and puts it in his pocket.

PATIENT: Who has taken the supplies we were sent from the west? Nurse?

FLORINA: I'm not on duty.

PATIENT: Did we have a revolution? Or what did we have?

RADU: Come on, let's find your bed.

Radu takes him off still talking.

PATIENT: Why did they close the schools a week early? Why did they evacuate the foreigners from the geriatric hospital? Who were the men in blue suits who appeared on the streets before the 21st?

Silence.

LUCIA: They have mental patients in here with the wounded? That's not very good.

FLORINA: He was wounded on the head. / He has

LUCIA: That explains a lot.

FLORINA: headaches and gets upset. Yes, he's a bit crazy.

Pause.

LUCIA: Hungarians were fighting beside us they said
on TV. And Ianoş wasn't hurt, that's good. I think
Americans like Hungarians.

GABRIEL: The poor Hungarians have a bad time because they're not treated better than everyone else.
How did they treat us when they had the chance? They
go abroad and insult Romania to make people despise
us.

LUCIA: This is what we used to say before. Don't we
say something different?

GABRIEL: Ask granny about Hungarians.

LUCIA: It's true, in America they even like the idea of
gypsies, they think how quaint. But I said to them you
don't like blacks here, you don't like hispanics, we're
talking about lazy greedy crazy people who drink too
much and get rich on the black market. That shut them
up.

GABRIEL: But Ianoş doesn't count as Hungarian.

Radu comes back.

LUCIA: So you got rid of the lunatic all right? Have
some more chocolate.

Radu shakes his head.

Go on, there's plenty more.

RADU: We're not greedy, Lucia. We don't just think about food.

LUCIA: It's a celebration, it's fun to have chocolate, can't you have fun?

RADU: No I can't. Celebrate what?

FLORINA: Radu, not now.

RADU: Who was shooting on the 22nd? That's not a crazy question.

FLORINA: Lucia's just arrived. Gabriel's still not well.

RADU: The only real night was the 21st. After that, what was going on? It was all a show.

LUCIA: No, it was real, Radu, / I saw it on television.

FLORINA: I don't want to hear / all this now.

RADU: Were they fighting or pretending to fight? Who let off firecrackers? Who brought loudhailers?

Pause.

Lucia looks at Florina.

FLORINA: At the Municipal Hospital the head doctor gave medical supplies for the west to the police to sell on the black market. / And

LUCIA: That I can believe.

RADU: he locked the wounded in a room with no one

to take care of them so he could hand them over / to
the Securitate and some of them died.

LUCIA: But that's just him. It's not a plot.

Pause.

FLORINA: How many people were killed at Timişoara?
Where are the bodies? There were bodies found in a
sandpit for the longjump. / Where are the rest?

LUCIA: But what does that mean?

RADU: Why did no one turn off the power at the TV
station?

Pause.

LUCIA: Gabriel? Rodica?

GABRIEL: I'm too tired.

Rodica turns her head away.

iv.

*Some time later, Irina helping Gabriel to walk. He reaches
a chair and falls into it laughing.*

IRINA: Good. Good.

Silence.

I used to say more with the radio on.

GABRIEL: Have you heard people say that by the 22nd
/ the revolution had been stolen?

IRINA: No no no no no. I've no time for all that non-
sense.

GABRIEL: But—

IRINA: No. No no no. Now. Walk.

**3. Rodica mai are coşmare. Rodica is still having
nightmares.**

*Rodica is wearing a cloak and a big fur hat with dollars
and flowers on it. Two soldiers come in.*

SOLDIER 1:   We're the last soldiers, your Majesty. The
rest of the army's on the side of the people.

SOLDIER 2:   The helicopter's going to rescue you.

*She takes a telephone from under her cloak and dials end-
lessly.*

*The Soldiers take off their uniforms and get dressed again
in each other's identical clothes. Meanwhile Gabriel comes
in wearing a huge Romanian flag, his head through the
hole. He gives Rodica a box of matches and goes.*

SOLDIER 2:   Why doesn't anyone love you after all
you've done for them?

SOLDIER 1:   Have you enough money to pay for the
helicopter?

She gives them money from her hat. They pocket each thing she gives them and hold out their hands for more till she has nothing left on her hat. She gives them the hat. They hold out their hands for more.

SOLDIER 1:   Give us your hands.

Her hands disappear under her cloak.

SOLDIER 2:   Give us your feet.

Her feet disappear under her cloak and she sinks down till she is kneeling.

SOLDIER 1:   There's no helicopter. You'll have to run.

The Soldiers go.

Rodica opens the matchbox—'ole ole ole ole' chanted by huge crowd. She opens and closes it several times and the song continues each time. Sound of gunfire. She looks round in a panic for somewhere to hide the matchbox. She puts it under her cloak, then changes her mind and takes it out. It is now a pill, which she swallows.

A Soldier comes in and searches, kicking at anything in the way.

He goes to her and opens her mouth.

'Ole ole ole ole' chanted by huge crowd.

He opens and closes her mouth several times, the chant continues each time.

4. Cînd am fost să ne vizităm bunicii la ţară, era o zi însorită. When we went to visit our grandparents in the country it was a sunny day.

Florina, Lucia, Radu and Ianoş are visiting Florina and Lucia's Grandparents in the country, so they can meet Radu before the wedding. The Grandparents are peasants. Ianoş has a child with him, a boy of about 8, Toma. The following things happen in the course of a long sunny afternoon, out of doors, immediately outside the Grandparents' house where there is a bench, and nearby.

i.

The Grandparents embrace Lucia and Florina, greet Radu warmly, Ianoş more formally. Toma clings shyly to Ianoş.

ii.

Ianoş has a ball and tries to interest Toma in playing with him and Radu. They go off.

GRANDMOTHER: That young man's a Hungarian.

LUCIA: He's a friend of Radu and Gabriel's, granny.

GRANDMOTHER: I knew a woman married a Hungarian. His brother killed her and ripped the child out of her stomach.

FLORINA: He's just a friend of Gabriel's, granny.

GRANDMOTHER: Radu seems a nice young man. He's Romanian. What's wrong with that child?

FLORINA: He's been in an orphanage.

GRANDMOTHER: Is it a gypsy?

LUCIA: Of course not.

GRANDMOTHER: They wouldn't let him adopt a Romanian.

iii.

Lucia with Ianoş and Toma.

LUCIA: Do we have to have him with us all the time?

IANOŞ: He likes me.

LUCIA: I like you but I'm not getting much chance to show it.

IANOŞ: He'll settle down.

LUCIA: Can he talk?

IANOŞ: Yes of course.

LUCIA: I haven't heard him.

IANOŞ: He doesn't know you.

LUCIA: I think your parents are remarkable. What if it goes wrong? Can you give him back?

IANOŞ: We don't want to give him back. We're adopting him.

LUCIA: Your parents are adopting him.

IANOŞ: Yes but me too.

Lucia rolls the ball.

LUCIA: Don't you want to play with the ball, Toma?

She goes and gets it herself.

Ball. Ball. Can you say ball, Toma?

Toma buries himself in Ianoş.

LUCIA: I think your parents are sentimental.

IANOŞ: Are you going back to America?

Lucia shrugs.

I still owe your husband money.

LUCIA: Did you borrow money from him?

IANOŞ: He paid for the abortion.

LUCIA: But he didn't know. It was money he gave me, it was my money. You can't pay him back, he'd want to know what it was for.

IANOŞ: I haven't got the money anyway.

Pause.

Aren't you ashamed?

LUCIA: What of? No.

IANOŞ: Not the abortion.

LUCIA: What?

IANOŞ: I don't know. The wedding?

LUCIA: No, why?

IANOŞ: I'm ashamed.

LUCIA: Why?

Pause.

IANOŞ: I'm ashamed of loving you when I think you're
probably not very nice.

Silence.

LUCIA: Shall I stay here and marry you?

Silence.

This is the last of the chocolate.

*As she gets it out, Toma pounces on it and runs a little way
off, stuffing it all into his mouth.*

You horrible child. I hate you.

IANOŞ: Don't shout at him. How can he help it? You're
so stupid.

LUCIA: Don't shout at me.

Toma whimpers. He starts to shake his head obsessively.

IANOȘ: Toma. Come here.

Toma goes on.

Ianoș goes to him.

Toma.

Toma hits Ianoș and starts to bellow with panic. Ianoș holds him, he subsides into whimpering. Ianoș sits on the ground holding him.

LUCIA: Did you tell anyone about us after I left?

IANOȘ: No.

LUCIA: It might be better if we're seen as something new.

Silence.

LUCIA: Is he very naughty?

IANOȘ: Not yet. Most of the time he's so good it's frightening. The babies there don't cry.

LUCIA: He's going to be terrible. I won't be much use.

Silence.

IANOȘ: I'd like to go to America. I've got a passport.

LUCIA: Just for a holiday. I don't like America.

IANOȘ: So is that the only reason you want to stay here? I hoped you loved America.

Pause.

Would your family let you marry a Hungarian?

iv.

Radu and Florina. Radu drawing.

RADU: Iliescu's going to get in because the workers and peasants are stupid.

Pause.

Not stupid but they don't think. They don't have the information.

Pause.

I don't mean your family in particular.

FLORINA: You're a snob like your father. You'd have joined the party.

RADU: Wouldn't you?

Silence.

He touches her face.

FLORINA: I used to feel free then.

RADU: You can't have.

FLORINA: I don't now and I'm in a panic.

RADU: It's because the Front tricked us. / When we've got rid—

FLORINA: It's because I could keep everything out.

Pause.

RADU: But you didn't have me then.

FLORINA: No but I thought you were perfect.

RADU: I am perfect.

Silence.

RADU: What?

FLORINA: Sometimes I miss him.

RADU: What? Why?

FLORINA: I miss him.

RADU: You miss hating him.

FLORINA: Maybe it's that.

RADU: I hate Iliescu.

FLORINA: That's not the same.

RADU: I hate him worse. Human face. And he'll get in because they're stupid and do what they're told. Ceauşescu Ceauşescu. Iliescu Iliescu.

FLORINA: I don't have anyone to hate. You sometimes.

RADU: Me?

FLORINA: Not really.

RADU: Me?

v.

The Grandparents are sitting side by side on the bench, the others around them. The Grandparents speak slowly, the others fast.

GRANDFATHER: He was killed while he was putting up posters.

RADU: You see? they're murderers. / It's the same

LUCIA: For which party, grandpa?

RADU: tactics / of intimidation.

IANOŞ: Who killed him?

GRANDFATHER: Posters for the Peasants Party.

FLORINA: Is that / who you support?

RADU: The Front claim the country supports them but it's only / because of intimidation.

IANOŞ: So did they find out who killed him?

GRANDMOTHER: Yes, it was gypsies killed him.

RADU: Gypsies? / They were probably paid by the

FLORINA: How did they know it was them?

RADU: Front.

IANOȘ: They'd hardly need paying to murder somebody.

RADU: Or it could have been Front supporters /

LUCIA: Or Securitate.

RADU: and they put the blame on the gypsies.

GRANDFATHER: It was two gypsies, a father and son,
who used to work in his garden. They had a quarrel
with him. He used to beat them.

LUCIA: So was it just a quarrel, / not politics at all?

FLORINA: Did anyone see them?

GRANDMOTHER: But that quarrel was years ago.

GRANDFATHER: A lot of people didn't like him because he used to be a big landowner. The Peasants
Party would give him back his land.

FLORINA: So was he killed because / the rest of the

LUCIA: I thought the Peasants Party was for peasants.

IANOȘ: No, they're millionaires the leaders of it.

FLORINA: village didn't want him to get all the land?

LUCIA: He should get it / if it's his.

FLORINA: No after all this time working on it / everyone—

RADU: Never mind that, he was against the Front, that's why they killed him. He was against the Communists.

GRANDFATHER: He was a party member. He was very big round here. He was a big Securitate man.

LUCIA: So whose side was he on?

GRANDMOTHER: He wasn't a nice man. Nobody liked him.

vi.

Grandfather is sitting on the bench, the others lying on the grass, each separately except that Toma is near Ianoş. Long silence.

IANOŞ: I want to go to Peru.

RADU: Rome. And Pompeii.

LUCIA: A holiday by the sea.

Pause

FLORINA: Sleep late in the morning.

Pause.

RADU: Paint what I see in my head.

FLORINA: Go into work tomorrow and everyone's better.

LUCIA: Gabriel walking.

IANOŞ: Rodica talking.

They laugh.

FLORINA: New shoes.

RADU: Paintbrushes with fine points.

Pause.

FLORINA: Drive a fast car.

LUCIA: Be famous.

IANOŞ: Toblerone.

Pause.

RADU: Make money.

Pause.

IANOŞ: Learn everything in the world by the end of the week.

Pause.

LUCIA: Not be frightened.

The pauses get longer.

RADU: Make Florina happy.

Long pause.

IANOŞ: Make Toma happy.

Silence.

FLORINA: Live forever.

Longer silence.

LUCIA: Die young.

Very long silence.

FLORINA: Go on lying here.

Very long silence.

5. Mai doreşti puţină brînză? Would you like some more cheese?

Mihai and Flavia eating cheese and salami.

FLAVIA: You know when Radu was born and they said he'd be born dead. Three days, no hope. And then Radu. The pain stops just like that. And then joy. I felt the same the morning of the 22nd. Did you ever feel joy before?

MIHAI: I'm not sure I did.

FLAVIA: All those years of pain forgotten. You felt that?

MIHAI: It was certainly a remarkable experience.

FLAVIA: It can't last of course. Three days after he was born I was crying. But I still loved Radu. And what have we still got from the 22nd?

MIHAI: The work on the People's Palace will probably continue as soon as its new function has been determined.

FLAVIA: What?

MIHAI: If not I'm sure they'll find me some other work. I'm not in any way compromised, I was on the streets, I'm clearly a supporter of the Front. And in any case—

FLAVIA: I wasn't talking about you.

MIHAI: Good, I had the impression you might be worried.

Pause.

FLAVIA: All I was trying to do was teach correctly. Isn't history what's in the history book? Let them give me a new book, I'll teach that.

MIHAI: Are you losing your job?

FLAVIA: I didn't inform on my pupils, I didn't accept bribes. Those are the people whose names should be on the list.

MIHAI: Are they not on the list?

FLAVIA: They are on the list but why am I with them?
The new head of department doesn't like me. He
knows I'm a better teacher than he is. I can't stop
teaching, I'll miss the children.

Silence during which Radu comes in.

Why are you always out, Radu? Come and eat.

Radu is already making sandwiches.

MIHAI: I hope you're going to join us for a meal.

Radu goes on making sandwiches.

RADU: Have you noticed the way Iliescu moves his
hands? And the words he uses?

MIHAI: He comes from a period when that was the
style.

RADU: Yes, he does, doesn't he.

MIHAI: Not tonight, Radu. Your mother's had bad
news at work about her job.

FLAVIA: The new head of department—

RADU: There you are. It's because of me. No one who's
opposed to the Front / will get anywhere.

MIHAI: Radu, I don't know what to do with you. Nothing is on a realistic basis.

RADU: Please don't say that.

MIHAI: What's the matter now?

RADU: Don't say 'realistic basis.'

FLAVIA: It's true, Mihai, you do talk in terrible jargon from before, it's no longer correct.

MIHAI: The head of department is in fact a supporter of the Liberals.

RADU: Is he?

FLAVIA: It may not come to anything.

RADU: You mean it's because of what you did before? What did you do?

MIHAI: Radu, this is not a constructive approach.

RADU: It won't come to anything, don't worry. It's five weeks since we made our list of bad teachers. Nobody cares that the students and staff voted. It has to go to the Ministry.

FLAVIA: Do you want me to lose my job?

RADU: If you deserve to.

Flavia slaps Radu

Silence.

RADU: Do you remember once I came home from school and asked if you loved Elena Ceauşescu?

FLAVIA: I don't remember, no. When was that?

RADU: And you said yes. I was seven.

FLAVIA: No, I don't remember.

Pause.

But you can see now why somebody would say what they had to say to protect you.

RADU: I've always remembered that.

FLAVIA: I don't remember.

RADU: No, you wouldn't.

Pause.

FLAVIA: Why are you saying this, Radu? Are you making it up? You're manipulating me to make me feel bad. I told you the truth about plenty of things.

RADU: I don't remember.

FLAVIA: No, you wouldn't.

Silence.

Now. We have some dried apples.

RADU: I expect dad got them from someone with a human face.

Radu is about to leave.

MIHAI: Radu, how do you think you got into the Art Institute?

RADU: The still life with the green vase was the one /
they particularly—

MIHAI: Yes your work was all right. I couldn't have
managed if it was below average.

Radu leaves Mihai with the sandwiches and goes. Silence.

MIHAI: Who do we know who can put in a word for
you?

FLAVIA: We don't know who we know. Someone who
put in a word before may be just the person to try and
keep clear of.

Pause.

But Radu's painting is exceptional.

MIHAI: Yes, in fact I didn't do anything.

FLAVIA: You must tell him.

MIHAI: He won't believe me.

Pause.

FLAVIA: Twenty years marching in the wrong direction. I'd as soon stop. Twenty years' experience and I'm
a beginner. Yes, stop. There, I feel better. I'm not a
teacher.

MIHAI: They might just transfer you to the provinces.

Pause.

It won't happen. Trust me.

Silence. Mihai goes on with his meal.

FLAVIA: Granny. Granny?

Her Grandmother doesn't come. Silence.

Flavia goes on with her meal.

6. Gabriel vine acasă diseară. Gabriel is coming home tonight.

Downstairs in the block of flats where Gabriel and Rodica live. Gabriel, with a crutch, is arriving home from hospital with Radu, Florina, Lucia, Ianoş, and other friends. They have been for a drink on the way and have some bottles with them.

ALL: The lift's broken.
How do we get Gaby up the stairs?
We'll have the party here.
Rodica's waiting in the flat.
We shouldn't have stayed so long at the Berlin.
We can carry him up.
We need a drink first.
Let's do it here.
Do it, I've never seen it.
Yes, Radu, to celebrate Gaby coming home.

Someone announces:

The trial and execution of Nicolae and Elena Ceauşescu.

Radu and Florina are the Ceauşescus.

IANOŞ: Hurry up. Move along.

RADU: Where are they taking us, Elena?

FLORINA: I don't know, Nicu. He's a very rude man.

RADU: Don't worry we'll be rescued in a minute. This is all part of my long-term plan.

Ceauşescu (Radu) keeps looking at his watch and up at the sky.

IANOŞ: Sit down.

FLORINA: Don't sit down.

RADU: My legs are tired.

FLORINA: Stand up.

IANOŞ: Sit down.

RADU: The Securitate will get in touch with my watch.

IANOŞ: Answer the questions of the court.

RADU: What court? I don't see any court. Do you, Elena?

FLORINA: No court anywhere here.

RADU: The only judges I recognise are ones I've appointed myself.

SOMEONE: You're on trial for genocide.

FLORINA: These people are hooligans. They're in the pay of foreign powers. That one's just come back from America.

ALL: Who gave the order to shoot at Timişoara?
What did you have for dinner last night?
Why have you got gold taps in your bathroom?
Do you shit in a gold toilet?
Shitting yourselves now.
Why did you pull down my uncle's house?
etc.

FLORINA: Where's the helicopter?

RADU: On its way.

FLORINA: Have these people arrested and mutilated.

RADU: Maybe just arrested and shot. They are our children.

FLORINA: After all we've done for them. You should kiss my hands. You should drink my bathwater.

ALL: That's enough trial.
We find you guilty on all counts.
Execution now.

FLORINA: You said there'd be a helicopter, Nicu.

IANOŞ: Stand up.

FLORINA: Sit down.

They are roughly pushed to another place.

RADU: You can't shoot me. I'm the one who gives the orders to shoot.

FLORINA: We don't recognise being shot.

ALL: Gypsy.
Murderer.
Illiterate.
We've all fucked your wife.
We're fucking her now.
Let her have it.

They all shoot Elena (Florina), who falls dead at once. Gabriel, who is particularly vicious throughout this, shoots with his crutch. All make gun noises, then cheer. Ceauşescu (Radu) runs back and forth. They shout again.

ALL: We fucked your wife.
Your turn now.
Murderer.
Bite your throat out.

Meanwhile Ceauşescu (Radu) is pleading.

RADU: Not me, you've shot her that's enough, I've money in Switzerland, I'll give you the number of my bank account, you can go and get my money—

IANOŞ: In his legs.

They shoot and he falls over, still talking and crawling about.

RADU: My helicopter's coming, you'll be sorry, let me
go to Iran—

IANOŞ: In the belly.

They shoot, he collapses further but keeps talking.

RADU: I'll give you the People's Palace—

IANOŞ: In the head.

They shoot again. He lies still.

They all cheer and jeer.

Ceauşescu (Radu) sits up.

RADU: But am I dead?

ALL: Yes.

He falls dead again.

More cheering, ole ole ole etc.

Radu and Florina get up, everyone's laughing.

Ianoş hugs Lucia lightly.

Gabriel suddenly hits out at Ianoş with his crutch.

GABRIEL: Get your filthy Hungarian hands off her.

IANOŞ: What?

GABRIEL: Just joking.

A Man looks out of one of the doors of the flats to see what the noise is. They go quiet. He shuts the door.

7. Abia terminase lucrul, cînd a venit Radu. She had just finished work when Radu came.

Hospital at night. A corridor. Florina has just come off duty. Radu is meeting her. They hug.

FLORINA: Someone died tonight. It was his fifth operation. When they brought him in all the nurses were in love with him. But he looked like an old man by the time he died.

RADU: Was he one of the ones shot low in the back and out through the shoulder?

FLORINA: He was shot from above in the shoulder and it came out low down in his back.

RADU: No, all those wounds are / from being—

FLORINA: You don't know anything about it. I was nursing him.

RADU: A doctor told me.

FLORINA: What does it matter? / He's dead anyway.

RADU: They were in the crowd with us shooting people in the back.

Pause.

And where are they now?

Pause.

FLORINA: So what have you done today? Sat in the square and talked?

RADU: I know you're tired.

FLORINA: I like being tired, I like working, I don't like listening to you talk.

RADU: People are talking about a hunger strike.

FLORINA: Fine, those of you who weren't killed can kill yourselves.

Pause.

RADU: Do you want to know what it's for?

FLORINA: No.

Pause.

I hope you're not thinking of it.

RADU: Someone's been getting at you, haven't they?

FLORINA: Because if you do / the wedding's off.

RADU: Someone's threatened you. Or offered you something.

FLORINA: It's what I think. / Did you really say that?

RADU: I don't like what you think.

FLORINA: I don't like what you think. You just want to
go on playing hero, / you're weak, you're lazy—

RADU: You're betraying the dead. Aren't you ashamed?
Yes, I'm a hooligan. Let's forget we know each other. /
Communist.

FLORINA: You don't know me.

Radu goes.

Florina is alone.

She is joined by the Ghost of a young man.

GHOST: I'm dead and I never got married. So I've
come to find somebody. I was always looking at you
when I was ill. But you loved Radu then. I won't talk
like he does. I died, that's all I want to know about it.
Please love me. It's lonely when you're dead. I have to
go down a secret road. Come with me. It's simple.

8. Multă fericire. We wish you happiness.

*Florina and Radu's wedding party at a hotel. Both families
are there, and an old peasant Aunt of Bogdan's and a
Waiter. Music in background. The following conversations
take place, sometimes overlapping or simultaneously.*

i.

*It's some time in to the party so everyone's had a few
drinks without being drunk yet.*

1.

FLAVIA: What's so wonderful about a wedding is everyone laughs and cries and it's like the revolution again. Because everyone's gone back behind their masks. Don't you think so?

BOGDAN: I don't know. Perhaps. You could say that.

2.

MIHAI: I forgot to take my windscreen wipers off last night so of course they were stolen. Still, my son doesn't get married every day.

3.

IRINA: She and her followers talk without speaking, they know each other's thoughts. She just looks at you and she knows your troubles. I told her all about Gaby.

LUCIA: So you told her your troubles. No wonder she knows.

IRINA: When they send him to Italy for his operation maybe we won't need a clairvoyant. She said I could take him to see her.

LUCIA: He'll just laugh.

IRINA: She says we have no soul. We've suffered for so many years and we don't know how to live. Are people very different in other countries, Lucia?

LUCIA: Cheer up, have a drink. It's Florina's wedding day.

IRINA: I'll miss Florina.

4.

Lucia is talking to a smiling Waiter.

WAITER: I remember your wedding last year. That
was a very different time. We had bugs in the vases.
Mind you. Can I help you change some dollars?

LUCIA: No thank you.

WAITER: I used to help your husband. It's easier now.
My brother's gone to Switzerland to buy a Mercedes.
You're sure I can't help you? Top rate, high as Everest.

LUCIA: Thank you but I've no dollars left.

The Waiter's smile disappears.

5.

BOGDAN: I know someone at work killed his son-in-
law. He put an axe in his head. Then he put a knife in
the dead man's hand to make out it was self-defence,
and said anyway he wasn't there, it was his son. And he
got away with it. Clever eh?

RADU: What happened to the son?

BOGDAN: Luckily he had some money, he only got six
years.

RADU: What's he going to do to his dad when he gets
out?

They laugh.

6.

FLAVIA: How's your little brother?

IANOŞ: He wakes up in the night now and cries.

FLAVIA: How's your mother?

They laugh.

7.

FLORINA: I thought I was going to get the giggles.

RADU: It was good though.

FLORINA: It was lovely.

8.

IANOŞ: Lucia and I are going to start a newspaper.

LUCIA: A friend's sending us magazines from America
     and we'll translate interesting articles.

IANOŞ (*to Lucia*):   Do people really dress like in Vogue?

9.

IRINA: I bought these shoes in the street.

FLAVIA: Did they want dollars?

IRINA: Yes, Lucia's last dollars went on the wedding.

FLAVIA: Black market prices have shot up.

IRINA: It's not black market, it's free market.

10.

IANOŞ: A French doctor told me 4000 babies / have it.

GABRIEL: I hate the French, they're so superior.

IANOŞ: Yes, they do like to help.

GABRIEL: Merci, merci.

IANOŞ: Can you really sterilise infected needles with alcohol?

GABRIEL: I'm sterilising myself with alcohol.

11.
Old peasant Aunt shouts ritual chants at Florina.
AUNT: Little bride, little bride,
   You're laughing, we've cried.
   Now a man's come to choose you
   We're sad because we lose you.
   Makes you proud to be a wife
   But it's not an easy life.
   Your husband isn't like a brother
   Your mother-in-law's not like a mother.
   More fun running free and wild
   Than staying home to mind a child.
   Better to be on the shelf
   Only have to please yourself.
   Little bride don't be sad,
   Not to marry would be mad.
   Single girls are all in tears,
   They'll be lonely many years.
   Lovely girl you're like a flower, /
   Only pretty for an hour—

BOGDAN: Hush, auntie, you're not in the country now.

FLORINA: No, I like it. Go on.

ii.

*Later. People have had more to drink and are more cheer-
ful, emotional, aggressive.*

1.
IRINA: If only he'd stayed in University Square.

LUCIA: He could have been shot there.

IRINA: The bullets missed Ianoş.

LUCIA: Do you wish they'd hit him?

IRINA: No but of course anyone else.

2.
FLORINA: Be nice to your mum and dad.

RADU: I am nice.

3.
BOGDAN: Whinge whinge. Gaby was shot, all right.
Everyone whinges. Layabout students. Radu and Ianoş
never stop talking, want to smack them in the mouth.
'Was it a revolution?' Of course it was. / My son was
shot for it and we've got

MIHAI: Certainly.

BOGDAN: This country needs a strong man.

MIHAI: And we've got one.

BOGDAN: We've got one. Iliescu's a strong man. We can't have a traffic jam forever. Are they going to clear the square or not?

MIHAI: The government has to avoid any action that would give credibility to the current unsubstantiated allegations.

BOGDAN: They're weak, aren't they.

4.

FLAVIA: I'm going to write a true history, Florina, so we'll know exactly what happened. How far do you think Moscow was involved / in planning the coup?

FLORINA: I don't know. I don't care. I'm sorry.

FLAVIA: What did you vote? Liberal?

FLORINA: Yes of course.

FLAVIA: So did I, so did I.

She hugs Florina.

Mihai doesn't know. And next time we'll win. Jos Iliescu.

5.

RADU: Look at Gaby, crippled for nothing. They've voted the same lot in.

IRINA: It's thanks to Gaby you can talk like this.

6.

JANOS: Have another drink.

LUCIA: I've had another drink.

JANOS: Have another other drink.

They laugh.

7.

IRINA: Ceauşescu shouldn't have been shot.

RADU: Because he would have exposed people / in the Front.

IRINA: He should have been hung up in a cage and stones thrown at him.

They laugh.

8.

BOGDAN (*to Mihai*):   If Radu had been hurt instead of Gaby, he'd be in hospital in Italy by now.

9.

GABRIEL: I can't work. Rodica can't work. What's going to happen to us? I wish I'd been killed.

FLORINA: You're going to Italy.

GABRIEL: When? Can't you do something to hurry things up, Florina? Sleep with a doctor? Just joking.

10.

IRINA: I don't like seeing you with Ianoş.

LUCIA: He's Gabriel's friend.

IRINA: I was once in a shop in Transylvania and they
wouldn't serve me because I couldn't speak Hungarian.
/ In my own country.

LUCIA: Yes, but—

IRINA: And what if the doctor only spoke Hungarian /
and someone wanted a doctor?

BOGDAN: Stuck-up bastards.

IRINA: Are you going back to America? You're not going back.

LUCIA: Didn't you miss me?

IRINA: Aren't you ashamed? Two years of hell to get
your precious American and you don't even want him.
Did he beat you?

LUCIA: I got homesick.

IRINA: Was Ianoş going on before?

LUCIA: Of course not. You didn't think that?

IRINA: I don't know what I thought. I just made the
wedding dress.

LUCIA: You like Ianoş.

IRINA: Go back to America, Lucia, and maybe we can
all go. You owe us that.

BOGDAN: You're a slut, Lucia.

11.
FLAVIA: Where are the tapes they made when they
listened to everyone talking? All that history wasted.
I'd like to find someone in the Securitate who could tell
me. Bogdan, do you know anyone?

BOGDAN: Why me?

FLAVIA: I used to know someone but she's disap-
peared.

BOGDAN: They should be driven into the open and
punished. Big public trials. The Front aren't doing their
job.

FLAVIA: There wouldn't be enough prisons.

BOGDAN (*to Mihai*):   There's a use for your People's
Palace.

12.
MIHAI: I was in the British Embassy library reading
the Architect's Journal and there's a building in Japan
forty stories high with a central atrium up to twenty
stories. So the problem is how to get light into the
central volume. The German engineer has an ingenious
solution where they've installed computerised mirrors
angled to follow the sun so they reflect natural light
into the atrium according to the season and the time of
day, so you have sunlight in a completely enclosed
space.

13.
FLORINA: I'm glad about you and Ianoş.

They kiss.

   Tell me something.

LUCIA: Don't ask.

FLORINA: No, tell me.

LUCIA: Two years is a long time when you hardly know
   somebody. I'd lost my job, I had to go through with it,
   I wanted to get away.

FLORINA: But you loved Wayne at first? If you didn't
   I'll kill you.

LUCIA: Of course I did. But don't tell Ianoş.

14.
PRIEST: You can't blame anybody. Everyone was trying to survive.

BOGDAN: Wipe them out. Even if it's the entire popu-
   lation. We're rubbish. The Front are stuck-up bastards.
   They'd have to wipe themselves out too.

PRIEST: We have to try to love our enemies.

BOGDAN: Plenty of enemies. So we must be the most
   loving people in the world. Did you love him? Give
   him a kiss would you?

PRIEST: When I say love. It's enough not to hate.

BOGDAN: Handy for you having God say be nice to Ceauşescu.

PRIEST: You're your own worst enemy, Bogdan.

BOGDAN: So I ought to love myself best.

PRIEST: Don't hate yourself anyway.

BOGDAN: Why not? Don't you? You're a smug bugger.

iii.

Later. Two simultaneous conversations develop so that there are two distinct groups. Everyone has drunk a lot by now. Bogdan, who is too drunk to care if anyone listens, puts remarks at random to either group.

1.
BOGDAN: Private schools, private hospitals. I've seen what happens to old people. I want to buy my father a decent death.

b. I support the Peasants Party because my father's a peasant. I'm not ashamed of that. They should have their land because their feet are in the earth and they know things nobody else knows. Birds, frogs, cows, god, the direction of the wind.

c. CIA, KGB, we're all in the hands of foreign agents. That's one point where I'm right behind Ceauşescu.

2.

Mihai, Radu and Florina, joined by Flavia.

MIHAI: The Front wouldn't fix the vote because they
   knew they were going to win. Everyone appreciates
   the sacrifice made by youth. The revolution is in safe
   hands. This isn't a day for worrying, Florina and Radu,
   you take too much on yourselves. I wish you could let
   it all go for a little while. Please believe me, I want
   your happiness.

FLORINA: We know you do.

She kisses him.

RADU: Yes, I know. I appreciate that.

MIHAI: After all, I'm not a monster. Most of the country supports the Front. It's only in my own home it
   takes courage to say it. We have a government of recon-
   ciliation.

FLAVIA: Why don't the Front tell the truth and admit
   they're communists? / * Nothing to be

MIHAI: Because they're not.

RADU: * I don't care what they're called, it's the same
   people.

FLAVIA: ashamed of in communism, / nothing to be

FLORINA: They should have been banned / from

MIHAI: That's your idea of freedom, banning people?

FLORINA: standing in the election.

RADU: We've got to have another revolution.

FLAVIA: ashamed of in planning the revolution if
they'd just admit it. You never dared speak out against
Ceauşescu, Mihai, and you don't dare speak out now.
Say it, I'm a communist and so what. / Say it, I'm a
communist.

RADU: Jos comunismul, jos comunismul. / Jos Iliescu.
Jos tiranul. Jos Iliescu. Jos Iliescu.

FLORINA: Radu, don't be childish.

*Bogdan joins in shouting 'Jos comunismul,' then turns his
attention to the other group.*

3.
*Gabriel at first in group with Mihai then with Lucia, Ianoş
and Irina.*

GABRIEL: The only reason we need an internal secu-
rity force is if Hungary tried to invade us / we'd need to
be sure—

LUCIA: Invade? are you serious?

IANOŞ: When we get Transylvania back it's going to be
legally / because it's ours.

IRINA: You're not going to marry a Hungarian.

LUCIA: I'm married already.

IANOŞ: Gaby, the Hungarians started the revolution.

Without us you'd still be worshipping Ceauşescu. / And
now the

Gabriel jeers

LUCIA: We didn't worship him.

IRINA: Gaby's a hero, Ianoş.

IANOŞ: Romanians worship Iliescu. Who's the opposition? Hungarians.

GABRIEL: That's just voting for your language.

LUCIA: Why shouldn't they have their own schools?

IRINA: And lock Romanian children out in the street. If
it wasn't bad enough you going to America, now a
Hungarian, / and Gaby crippled, and Radu's irresponsible, I worry for Florina.

GABRIEL: If they want to live in Romania / they can

LUCIA: In the riots on TV I saw a Hungarian on the

GABRIEL: speak Romanian.

IANOŞ: We can learn two languages, we're not stupid.

LUCIA: ground and Romanians kicking him.

GABRIEL: That was a Romanian on the ground, and
Hungarians—you think we're stupid?

IANOŞ: You were under the Turks too long, it made you
like slaves.

LUCIA: You think I'm a slave? I'm not your slave.

Gabriel pushes Ianoş, who pushes him back. Bogdan arrives.

BOGDAN: Leave my son alone. Hungarian bastard. And don't come near my daughter.

IANOŞ: I'm already fucking your daughter, you stupid peasant.

Bogdan hits Ianoş.

Radu restrains Bogdan.

Lucia attacks Bogdan.

Bogdan hits Radu.

Mihai pushes Bogdan.

Bogdan hits Mihai.

Flavia attacks Bogdan.

Ianoş pushes Gabriel.

Irina protects Gabriel.

Gabriel hits Ianoş.

Radu attacks Bogdan.

Mihai restrains Radu.

Radu attacks Mihai.

Florina attacks Radu.

Gabriel hits out indiscriminately with his crutch and accidentally knocks Bogdan to the floor.

Stunned silence.

FLAVIA: This is a wedding. We're forgetting our programme. It's time for dancing.

They pick themselves up, see if they are all right. Music— the lambada. Gradually couples form and begin to dance. Bogdan and Irina, Mihai and Flavia, Florina and Radu, Lucia and Ianoș. Gabriel tries to dance on his crutch. For some time they dance in silence. The Angel and Vampire are there, dancing together. They begin to enjoy themselves.

Then they start to talk while they dance, sometimes to their partner and sometimes to one of the others, at first a sentence or two and finally all talking at once. The sentences are numbered in a suggested order. At 14, every couple talks at once, with each person alternating lines with their partner and overlapping with their partner at the end. So that by the end everyone is talking at once but leaving the vampire's last four or five words to be heard alone. At first they talk quietly then more freely, some angry, some exuberant. They speak Romanian.

BOGDAN: 1. Țara asta are nevoie de un bărbat puternic. (This country needs a strong man.)
5. Sîntem un gunoi. (We're rubbish.)
13. Dă-le una peste gură. (Smack them in the mouth.)
Ei știu lucruri pe care nimeni altcineva nu le știe, păsări, broaște, vaci, dumnezeu, direcția vîntului. (They

know things nobody else knows, birds, frogs, cows, god, the direction of the wind.)

IRINA: 3. Ea spune ca noi nu avem suflet. (She says we have no soul.)
12. (El) ar trebui spînzurat într-o cuşcă, să dea lumea cu pietre în el. (He should have been hung up in a cage and stones thrown at him.)
14. Tu n-o să te mariţi cu-n ungur. (You're not going to marry a Hungarian.) Datorită lui Gaby poţi să vorbeşti aşa. (It's thanks to Gaby you can talk like this.)

MIHAI: 8. Nimic nu e pe baze realistice. (Nothing is on a realistic basis.)
Trebuie să lăsăm trecutul în spate. (We have to put the past behind us.)
Frontul doreşte sa înlesnească democratia. (The Front wish to facilitate democracy.)
Ei nu vor aranja votarea, fiindcă ştiu ei că vor învinge. (They wouldn't fix the vote because they knew they were going to win.)

FLAVIA: 2. Nu este istoria ce e în cartea de istorie? (Isn't history what's in the history books?)
14. Vreau să predau corect. (I want to teach correctly.)
Unde sînt casetele? (Where are the tapes?)
Voi scrie o istorie adevarată, ca să ştim exact ce s-a întîmplat. (I'm going to write a true history so we'll know exactly what happened.)
Am votat cu liberalii. (I voted Liberal.)

FLORINA: 4. Uneori îmi este dor de el. (Sometimes I miss him.)
14. Doctorul şef a încuiat răniţii într-o cameră. (The head doctor locked the wounded in a room.)

Comuniştii nu trebuie să candideze în alegeri. (The communists shouldn't stand in the election.)
Imi place să fiu obosită, nu-mi place să te aud vorbind. (I like being tired, I don't like listening to you talk.)

RADU: 9. Cine a tras în douazeci şi doi? Nu e o întrebare absurdă. (Who was shooting on the 22nd? That's not a crazy question.)
Cine a aruncat pocnitori? Cine a adus difuzoare? (Who let off firecrackers? who brought loudhailers?)
Nu-mi pasă cum se numesc, este acelaşi popor. (I don't care what they're called it's the same people.)
Trădezi morţii. (You're betraying the dead.)

LUCIA: 11. Mi-a fost ruşine ca nu am fost acolo. (I was so ashamed not to be here.)
14. Dar ce inseamna asta? De ce parte a fost el? (But what does it mean? Whose side was he on?)
De ce n-au şcolile lor? (Why shouldn't they have their own schools?)
Nu sint sclava ta. (I'm not your slave.)

IANOŞ: 7. Eşti acuzat de genocid. (You're on trial for genocide.)
Cine este opozitia? Ungurii. (Who's the opposition? Hungarians.)
Voi aţi fost prea mult sub turci, sînţeti ca sclavii. (You were under the Turks too long, you're like slaves.)
Vreau sa invăţ tot. (I want to learn everything.)

GABRIEL: 10. Sînt aşa de fericit, ca sînt de cealaltă parte. (I'm so happy I've put myself on the other side.)
14. Diferit acum. (Different now.)
Ii urasc pe francezi. (I hate the French.)

Ungurii î fac pe oameni să ne dispreţuiască. (The
Hungarians make people despise us.)
Aş vrea să fi fost omorît. Glumesc. (I wish I'd been
killed. Just joking.)

ANGEL: 6. Să nu-ţi fie ruşine. (Don't be ashamed.)
13. Nu libertatea din afară ci libertatea interioară.
(Not outer freedom of course but inner freedom.)
Am încercat sa mă ţin departe de politică. (I try to
keep clear of the political side.)
Zburînd în albastru. (Flying about in the blue.)

VAMPIRE: 11. Nu-ţi fie frică. (Don't be frightened.)
14. Nu sînt o fiinţă umană. (I'm not a human being.)
Incepi sa vrei sînge. Membrele te dor, capul îţi arde.
Trebuie să te mişti din ce în ce mai repede. (You begin
to want blood. Your limbs ache, your head burns, you
have to keep moving faster and faster.)

THE SKRIKER

The Skriker was first performed in the Cottesloe auditorium of the Royal National Theatre, London, with the following cast. The first preview was held on 20 January 1994 and the press night on 27 January 1994.

THE SKRIKER	Kathryn Hunter
JOSIE	Sandy McDade
LILY	Jacqueline Defferary
PASSERBY	Desiree Cherrington
YALLERY BROWN	Don Campbell
BLACK DOG	Brian Lipson
KELPIE/FAIR FAIRY	Philippe Giraudeau
GREEN LADY/JENNIE GREENTEETH	Lucy Bethune
GIRL WITH TELESCOPE/ LOST GIRL	Melanie Pappenheim
HAG/WOMAN WITH KELPIE	Mary King
BOGLE/RAWHEADANDBLOODYBONES/ DARK FAIRY	Stephen Goff
BROWNIE/RADIANT BOY	Richard Katz
MAN WITH BUCKET/ NELLIE LONGARMS	Stephen Ley
SPRIGGAN	Robbie Barnett
GRANDDAUGHTER/BLACK ANNIS	Diana Payne Myers
GREAT-GREAT-GRANDDAUGHTER/ DEAD CHILD	Sarah Shanson

Director	Les Waters
Designer	Annie Smart
Music	Judith Weir
Movement	Ian Spink
Lighting	Christopher Toulmin

Characters

THE SKRIKER
JOSIE
LILY

JOSIE and LILY are in their late teens

JOHNNY SQUAREFOOT
THE KELPIE
MAN WITH CLOTH AND BUCKET
YALLERY BROWN
PASSERBY
GIRL WITH TELESCOPE
GREEN LADY
BOGLE
SPRIGGAN
WOMAN WITH KELPIE
BROWNIE
DEAD CHILD
FAIR FAIRY
DARK FAIRY
RAWHEADANDBLOODYBONES
BLACK DOG
NELLIE LONGARMS
JENNIE GREENTEETH
BLACK ANNIS
HAG
LOST GIRL
BUSINESSMEN
THRUMPINS
BLUE MEN
PICNIC FAMILY

GRANDDAUGHTER
GREAT-GREAT-GRANDDAUGHTER

This is the script as originally written, before the beginning of the rehearsal process. There may be divergences between this script and the play as staged at the Royal National Theatre.

A speech usually follows the one immediately before it, BUT:

1) When one character starts speaking before the other has finished, the point of interruption is marked / as in

JOSIE: They will / if you ask.

LILY: I don't think so.

2) A character sometimes continues speaking right through another's speech, e.g.:

LILY: Get away, you're crazy. / (*To Skriker.*) It's all

JOSIE: It's her.

SKRIKER: Mum, make her go away.

LILY: right. (*To Josie.*) I never want / to see you.

JOSIE: It's her.

THE SKRIKER

Underworld.

Johnny Squarefoot, a giant riding on a piglike man, throwing stones. He goes off.

The Skriker, a shapeshifter and death portent, ancient and damaged.

SKRIKER: Heard her boast beast a roast beef eater, daughter could spin span spick and spun the lowest form of wheat straw into gold, raw into roar, golden lion and lyonesse under the sea, dungeonesse under the castle for bad mad sad adders and takers away. Never marry a king size well beloved. Chop chip pan chap finger chirrup chirrup cheer up off with you're making no headway. Weeps seeps deeps her pretty puffy cream cake hole in the heart operation. Sees a little blackjack thingalingo with a long long tale awinding. May day, she cries, may pole axed me to help her. So I spin the sheaves shoves shivers into golden guild and geld and if she can't guessing game and safety match my name then I'll take her no mistake no mister no missed her no mist no miss no me no. Is it William Gwylliam Guillaume? Is it John Jack the ladder in your stocking is it Joke? Is it Alexander Sandro Andrew Drewsteignton? Mephistopheles Toffeenose Tiffany's Timpany Timothy Mossycoat? No 't ain't, says I, no tainted meat me after the show me what you've got. Then pointing her finger says Tom tit tot! Tomtom tiny tot blue tit tit! Out of her pinkle lippety loppety, out of her mouthtrap, out came my secreted garden flower of

my youth and beauty and the beast is six six six o'clock
in the morning becomes electric stormy petrel bomb.
Shriek! shrink! shuck off to a shack, sick, soak, seek a
sleep slope slap of the dark to shelter skelter away, a
wail a whirl a world away.

Slit slat slut. That bitch a botch an itch in my shoulder
blood. Bitch botch itch. Slat itch slit botch. Itch slut
bitch slit.

Put my hand to the baby and scissors seizures seize you
sizzle. Metal cross cross me out cross my heartburn
sunburn sunbeam in my eyelash your back. Or garlic
lickety split me in two with the stink bombastic. Or pin
prick cockadoodle do you feel it? But if the baby has no
name better nick a name, better Old Nick than no
name, because then we can have the snap crackle pop-
pet to bake and brew and broody more babies and
leave them an impossible, a gobbling, a no.

I've been a hairy here he is changeling changing chain-
saw massacre massive a sieve to carry water from the
well well what's to be done? Brother brewed beer in an
eggshell. I said I'm old old every so olden dazed but I
never see saw marjory before three two one blast off!

Put me on a red hot shovel pushel bushel and a peck
peck peck. Gave me red hot metal in a piping hot metal
in a pie ping pong what a stink. Call the vicar to exor-
cise exercise regular sex a size larger six or seventh
heaven and hellcat.

Chopped up the hag whole hog higgledy pig in the
middle. Kelpie gallops them into the loch stock and
barrel of fun fair enough and eats them, falls out of the
water into love with a ladylike, his head in her lap lap

lap, her hand in his hairy, there is sand in it there is and there is sand and shells shock. Bloody Bones hides in the dark dark dark we all go into the dark cupboard love all. See through the slit where he sits on piles of bloody boney was a warrior and chews whom he likes. Dollop gollop fullup.

But they're so fair fairy fair enough's as good as a feast day. Take them by the handle and dance in the fairy ring a ring ding sweet for a year and a day date data dated her and never finished the first reel first real dance in the fairy ring on your finger and bluebell would wouldn't it. Their friends drag 'em out dragon laying the country waste of time gentlemen. Listless and pale beyond the pale moonlight of heart sore her with spirits with spirit dancing the night away in a mangy no no no come back again.

Eating a plum in the enchanted orchard, cherry orchid, chanted orchestra was my undoing my doing my dying my undying love for you. Never eat a fruit or puck luck pluck a flower if you want to get back get your own back get back to your own back to the wall flower.

When did they do what they're told tolled a bell a knell, well ding dong pussy's in. Tell them one thing not to do, thing to rue won't they do it, boo hoo's afraid of the pig bag. Open bluebeard's one bloody chamber maid, eat the one forbidden fruit of the tree top down comes cradle and baby. Don't put your hand in the fountain pen and ink blot your copy catching fishes eyes and gluesniffer. So he puts his hand in and wail whale moby dictated the outcome into the garden maudlin. Everything gone with the window cleaner.

Don't get this ointment disappointment in your eyes I
say to the mortal middlewife but of course she does and
the splendoured thing palace picture palace winter po-
liceman's ball suddenly blurred visionary missionary
mishmash potato, and there was a mud hit mad hut and
the mother a murder in rags tags and bob's your uncle
and the baby a wrinkly crinkly crackerjack of all trading
places, because of course it was all a glamour amour
amorphous fuss about nothing. But she never lets on so
she gets home safe and sound the trumpet. But one day
I'm in the market with b and put it in the oven helping
myself and she sees me and says how's your wife waif
and stray how's the baby? And I say what eye do you
seize me with? This eye high diddley, she says. So I
point my finger a thing at her and strike her blind alley
cat o' nine tails.

Serve her right as raining cats and dogshit. Whatever
you do don't open the do don't open the door.

I got a sweet sucker sweet till it melts in your mouth.
Watched the bride a cock horse in her white lace cur-
tain up trip through the grieve grove graveyard rosy
and honeysuckle on her daddy's armour, lurked and
looked till the groom for one moribund strode up the
pathtime. Hold this candle the scandal I said, and he
stood till it gutterbed and went out. Then. What? No
wedding party frock! no broad no breed! no family life
jacket potato, no friends in need you ask! A hungered
yours hundred years later. And a bit a bite a bitter
bread and he was crumbs crumbling to dust panic.

Better forget them, not always be talking stalking walking working them over and understand still. Yes better
forgotten rotten leaves them alone. We don't need the
knock kneed knead the dough re mi fa away so there la

di da. Never think shrink so small about them at all a tall dark stranger than friction. Then stop cockadoodle if you cancan.

They used to leave cream in a sorcerer's apprentice. Gave the brownie a pair of trousers to wear have you gone? Now they hate us and hurt hurtle faster and master. They poison me in my rivers of blood poisoning makes my arm swelter. Can't get them out of our head strong.

Then get in their head body and tailor maiden has a perfect fit a frit a fright a frying tonight jar.

We'll be under the bedrock a bye and by. We'll follow you on the dark road at nightingale blowing. No but they're danger thin ice pick in your head long ago away. Blood run cold comfort me with apple pie. Roast cats alive alive oh dear what can the matterhorn piping down the valley wild horses wouldn't drag me.

Revengeance is gold mine, sweet. Fe fi fo fumbledown cottage pie crust my heart and hope to die. My mother she killed me and put me in pies for sale away and home and awayday. Peck out her eyes have it. I'll give you three wishy washy. An open grave must be fed up you go like dust in the sunlight of heart. Gobble gobble says the turkey turnkey key to my heart, gobbledegook de gook is after you. Ready or not here we come quick or dead of night night sleep tightarse.

Lily is visiting Josie in mental hospital. Lily is pregnant. Also there is the Kelpie, part young man, part horse.

JOSIE: I've a pain in my shoulder. I never used to have that did I. It's one of the things they give me here.

LILY: I don't remember.

Pause.

   Shall / I rub it?

JOSIE: The food's not healthy. They put two things the
   same colour like white fish and mash potato.

LILY: I could bring something in.

JOSIE: I'm here to be punished.

LILY: No, you were ill.

JOSIE: Yes and I'm better now so can I come home
   with you?

LILY: I don't think they'd let you.

JOSIE: They will / if you ask.

LILY: I don't think so.

Pause.

JOSIE: They will if you say you'll be responsible but
   you don't want to / be, do you.

LILY: They wouldn't anyway.

JOSIE: I don't blame you.

Pause.

All right, I will. I'll ask when I see the nurse. I'd love to take you out of here, Josie. I'd love it if I had a place of my own to take you and look after you, I'd love it.

JOSIE: Why?

LILY: Wouldn't you?

JOSIE: I wouldn't love it, no. I'd do it.

Pause.

LILY: Have you made any friends here?

JOSIE: I don't think so.

LILY: What are the nurses like?

JOSIE: I haven't noticed.

LILY: Do they do things to you? I won't ask if you don't want. Like electrocute you. Or put you in a padded / cell or—

JOSIE: They give me pills.

LILY: What sort? what you got?

JOSIE: That what you come for?

LILY: No but if you / got some—

JOSIE: I haven't got them, they've / got them.

LILY: Take more when they're not looking, bring a whole lot out, be a laugh.

JOSIE: You've no idea.

LILY: What? what have I no idea?

Pause.

   Nurse.

JOSIE: No.

LILY: What? Nurse.

JOSIE: No.

LILY: Don't you want to?

Pause.

   Was she being naughty?

JOSIE: You can't be naughty, a ten day old baby, can
   you. You really don't know anything / about

LILY: I just meant she might have annoyed you.

JOSIE: it. What can a ten day old baby do that's
   naughty?

LILY: Like crying or—I don't know.

JOSIE: You wouldn't kill a baby because it annoyed
   you, would you.

LILY: I don't know.

JOSIE: Would *you?*

LILY: I don't know. You tell me.

JOSIE: Of course you wouldn't.

Pause.

LILY: Was it difficult?

Pause.

JOSIE: Licence to kill, seems to me.

LILY: You're in here.

JOSIE: They don't hang you.

LILY: They don't hang anyone.

JOSIE: It should have been me that died.

LILY: No, why?

Pause.

It's nicer here than I expected. The garden.

JOSIE: You're thinking of going home.

LILY: Not right away, no, but—

JOSIE: Don't.

LILY: I'm not.

JOSIE: Take me with you.

LILY: Josie, listen. I'm going to run away. But I'll write
and tell you where I am, all right? I'm going to London.

JOSIE: I won't hurt your baby.

LILY: Of course not, I don't think that.

JOSIE: If you'd got any sense you would. But you'd be
wrong.

Pause.

Are you going then?

LILY: No.

Pause.

JOSIE: Wait till I tell you something.

Pause.

I thought it was a patient because if you saw them
you'd know what I mean, there's some of them I'm
nothing compared. You'd think I was worse because
I've done something but some of them think they're
someone else and I do know . . . What was I saying?

LILY: You thought someone was / a patient.

JOSIE: Yes but she's hundreds of years old. And then I
was impressed by the magic but now I think there's
something wrong with her.

LILY: When you say hundreds of years old, you mean like eighty?

JOSIE: She looks about fifty but she's I don't know maybe five hundred a million, I don't know how old these things are.

LILY: When you say magic?

JOSIE: I thought maybe she could go home with you.

LILY: Josie, you'll be coming out soon. It's better to wait till they say.

JOSIE: She'd like me to wish the baby back but I won't because she'd make it horrible.

LILY: How do you know she's not a patient who just thinks she's . . .

Pause.

JOSIE: Rub my shoulder.

Lily rubs Josie's shoulder.

LILY: When I get to the front gate is it left or right to the bus?

She goes on rubbing her shoulder. She stops.

All right?

Josie doesn't reply.

LILY: Josie?

Lily goes. Woman about 50 approaches. Dowdy, cardigan, could be a patient. It is the Skriker.

SKRIKER: I heard that.

JOSIE: What?

SKRIKER: You don't like me.

JOSIE: I'm thinking what you'd enjoy and you'd like her better than me. She's stronger, she's more fun. I'm ill and I think you're ill and I / don't think—

SKRIKER: You don't want me.

JOSIE: She'll have a baby and you'll like that.

SKRIKER: Please, please keep me.

Pause.

  I'll give you a wish.

JOSIE: I don't want a wish.

SKRIKER: I'll be nice.

JOSIE: It's cold all round you.

SKRIKER: I can get you out of here. Just say.

JOSIE: No. Where to? No.

SKRIKER: Josie.

JOSIE: All right, I'll have a wish.

SKRIKER: Yes? Wish.

JOSIE: I wish you'd have her instead of me.

Pause. Skriker turns away.

Wait. I don't mind you any more.

SKRIKER: No, I'm not after you.

JOSIE: You won't hurt her? What do you want from her?

Skriker starts to go. A Man comes in carrying a white cloth and a bucket of water.

Oh but I'll miss you now.

Skriker goes.

The Man spreads the cloth on the floor and stands the bucket of water on it. He waits. He isn't satisfied. He picks up the cloth and bucket and walks about looking for a better spot.

Meanwhile the Kelpie goes.

Yallery Brown is playing music.

The Man puts the cloth and bucket down in another place. A derelict woman is shouting in the street. It is the Skriker.

A Passerby comes along the street, throws down a coin, and then starts to dance to the music.

Lily comes along the street.

SKRIKER: What's the wires coming out of your head
for? Collecting his brain in a box, mind you don't lose
it. You've got a dead pig on your back.

She falls down in front of Lily. Lily helps her up.

Can you help a poor old lady, lost my bus pass, price of
a cup of tea, you've got a kind face darling, give you the
white heather another time.

*Lily gives her money and starts to go away but Skriker
holds her.*

The Man puts the cloth and bucket down in a new place.

Do I smell? It's my coat and my cunt. Give us a hug.
Nobody gives us a hug. Give us a kiss. Won't you give
us a hug and a kiss.

Lily suddenly hugs and kisses her.

There's a love. Off you go, Lily.

Skriker goes.

*The Man is satisfied with the position of cloth and bucket
and goes off without them.*

LILY: How do you know my name?—What? what's
happening? my teeth. I'm sick. Help me. What is it?
It's money. Is it? Out of my mouth?

*Pound coins come out of her mouth when she speaks. She
stops talking and examines the money.*

A Young Girl is looking through a telescope.

Lily speaks carefully, testing.

When I speak, does money come out of my mouth?
Yes.

Through the telescope The Girl sees a Green Lady danc-
ing with a Bogle.

The Passerby goes on dancing.

Lily goes.

A Young Man, who is a Brownie, comes in and starts
sweeping and cleaning.

The Green Lady and Bogle disappear when the girl looks
away from the telescope. The Girl looks again but they
don't reappear. The Girl goes.

The Passerby never stops dancing.

Skriker tells Lily's story.

SKRIKER: So lily in the pink with a finnyanny border
was talking good as gold speaking pound coins round
coins pouring roaring more and more, singing thinging
counting saying the alphabetter than nothing telling
stories more stories boring sore throat saw no end to it
fuckit buckets and buckets of bloodmoney is the root of
evil eye nose the smell hell the taste waste of money
got honey to swallow to please ease the sore throat so
could keep on talking taking aching waking all night to
reach retch wrench more and more and more on the
floor on the bed of a hotel tell me another not another
wish it would stop stop talking now and sleep at last
fast asleep and woke to find she can eek peak speak can

I speak without can I without and about now changing
the cash dash flash in the panic of time. And now in the
hotel bar none but the brave deserve a drink I think for
lily the

*Lily at a bar talking to an American woman of about 40
who is slightly drunk. It is the Skriker. There is a TV.*

*There is a Spriggan, grotesquely ugly and ten foot tall,
who is invisible to Lily, having a drink.*

*Later the Kelpie arrives. Then a Woman who drinks with
the Kelpie.*

*The Brownie goes on cleaning. Later he finishes work and
goes down on his hands and knees to lap a saucer of milk,
then goes.*

SKRIKER: So how does this work?

LILY: How?

SKRIKER: How does it—

LILY: You want to turn it off?

SKRIKER: No, how does that picture get here. From
wherever.

LILY: How does it *work?*

SKRIKER: Yes.

LILY: Oh you know, I don't know, you know, it's—isn't
it the same in America?

SKRIKER: Take your time. In your own words.

LILY: It has to be plugged in so it's got power, right, electricity, so it's on so you can turn it on when you press the button, so the light's on and that shows it's on, ok?

SKRIKER: But what's / the electricity—?

LILY: It's got all these tubes / and anyway—

SKRIKER: No how do you see / all over the world?

LILY: And meanwhile, let's say this is something live we're seeing, there's a camera there pointing at the picture at the thing that is the picture, camera, you want me to explain—the light gets in and there's the film, tape, the tape, it picks up the light somehow and it gets the picture *on* it, don't ask me, and there you are if it was a tape like you hire a tape down the video shop / that's it, they

SKRIKER: No, tell me.

LILY: make a whole lot of copies.

SKRIKER: It's happening *there* and it's / *here.*

LILY: I'm telling you, hang about, how it gets sent, I can't quite, through the air, if it's live, or even if it's not of course, if it happened before and they recorded—say it's live, it's coming—not the whole picture in the air obviously, it's in bits like waves like specks and you need an aerial / to

SKRIKER: This is crap.

LILY: catch it and this changes it back into the picture /
and it's not a solid thing, it's all dots

SKRIKER: But how for fuck's sake?

LILY: and lines if you look, I can't help it. If it's on the
other side of the world they bounce it off a satellite yes
I'm explaining satellite which is a thing a thing they put
up in space ok, they put it up I'm explaining that too
and it's going round like a star, stars don't go round,
like a moon but it looks like a star but moving about
you sometimes see it at night, and it bounces off the
satellite / all right—

SKRIKER: What bounces off?

LILY: The picture.

SKRIKER: The picture bounces off?

LILY: The waves, the—what is this?

SKRIKER: You're holding out on me.

LILY: I don't have all the technical if you want the
jargon if you want the detail you'll have to ask someone
else.

SKRIKER: Don't fuck with me.

LILY: Look, / that's all I—

SKRIKER: And flying. I suppose / you don't know

LILY: What?

SKRIKER: how you fly? / And the massive explosions that—

LILY: I don't fly.

SKRIKER: No idea, huh? Never fly, never flown / across the sea—

LILY: Fly you mean go in a plane no but even if I had / I wouldn't—

SKRIKER: Or how you make poisons?

LILY: What?

SKRIKER: You people are killing me, do you know that? I am sick, I am a sick woman. Keep your secrets, I'll find out some other way, I don't need to know these things, there are plenty of other things to know. Just so long as you know I'm dying, I hope that satisfies you to know I'm in pain.

LILY: Are you ill? Can I help? / Can I get something?

SKRIKER: No no no, forget it. Really.

LILY: You're in pain?

SKRIKER: Not at all, no, I'm just fine, forget it. I don't have much aptitude for science. I guess you don't either. No big deal. We can just watch what comes over.

Pause.

LILY: You feel all right?

SKRIKER: You are a sweet girl. You are just such a
sweet girl.

Pause.

Running away from home is a great start. I did it myself. It can get to be a habit. You keeping the baby?

LILY: Yes of course.

SKRIKER: Because I'm looking for one, no I'm kid-
ding. Look at it floating in the dark with its pretty
empty head upside down, not knowing what's waiting
for it. It's been so busy doubling doubling and now it's
just hovering nicely decorating itself with hair and toe-
nails. But once it's born it starts again, double double,
but this time the mind, think of the energy in that.
Maybe I could be the godmother.

LILY: You're staying in London?

SKRIKER: Do you have friends in London?

LILY: No but—

SKRIKER: You now have one friend in London. And I
have one friend in London. Ok? Not ok?

LILY: Yes yes I do want to be friends. I just—

Pause.

SKRIKER: Anyone would think you were frightened of
me. I'm frightened of you.

LILY: You're the one Josie said.

SKRIKER: But I want to be friends.

LILY: Why am I frightening?

SKRIKER: Lily, I'll level with you, ok? You ready for this? I am an ancient fairy, I am hundreds of years old as you people would work it out, I have been around through all the stuff you would call history, that's cavaliers and roundheads, Henry the eighth, 1066 and before that, back when the Saxons feasted, the Danes invaded, the Celts hunted, you know about any of this stuff? Alfred and the cakes, Arthur and the table, long before that, long before England was an idea, a country of snow and wolves where trees sang and birds talked and people knew we mattered, I don't to be honest remember such a time but I like to think it was so, it should have been, I need to think it, don't contradict me please. That's what I am, one of many, not a major spirit but a spirit.

LILY: And why are you here?

SKRIKER: I am here to do good. I am good. You look as if you doubt that.

LILY: No, of course not.

SKRIKER: I am a good fairy.

LILY: You do good magic?

SKRIKER: That's exactly what I do.

LILY: And you'll do it for me?

SKRIKER: Where do you think your money comes from?

LILY: I'm not ungrateful.

SKRIKER: You're the one I've chosen out of everyone in the world.

LILY: Why?

SKRIKER: Because you're beautiful and good. Don't you think you are? Yes everyone sometimes thinks they're beautiful and good and deserve better than this and so they do. Are you telling me I made a mistake? I'd be sorry to think I'd made a mistake.

LILY: No. No I'm glad.

SKRIKER: And you accept?

LILY: What?

SKRIKER: Accept my offer. Accept my help.

LILY: Yes. I think—what offer?

SKRIKER: My help.

LILY: Do I have to do something?

SKRIKER: Just accept my help, sweetheart.

Pause.

LILY: No, I . . . It's very kind of you but . . . I don't like to say no but . . .

SKRIKER: You might as well say yes. You can't get rid of me.

LILY: No.

SKRIKER: Who the fuck do you think you are?

Pause.

Whatever you say.

LILY: You should have stayed with Josie. She's braver than me.

SKRIKER: She wished I'd go with you.

LILY: Did she? I wish she'd come and help me then.

SKRIKER: That's the way. You'll begin to get a taste for it.

LILY: For what?

SKRIKER: Wishes.

LILY: I didn't—

SKRIKER: Yes.

Pause.

Tell me how the TV works and I'll trade.

LILY: I don't know how the TV works.

SKRIKER: Would you like a ring that when you look at
the stone you can tell if your loved one is faithful?

LILY: I don't have a loved one.

SKRIKER: I can fix that, no problem. Just tell me how /
the TV—

LILY: I don't know how the TV works.

Lily goes.

The Woman gets on the Kelpie's back and rides off.

Spriggan goes. Skriker goes.

*The Man comes back to his bucket and cloth. He skims a
gold film off the top of the water in the bucket which he
makes into a cake. He puts the cake on the cloth, draws a
circle around it and sits down to wait. The Passerby is still
dancing.*

A Dead Child sings.

DEAD CHILD:
My mother she killed me and put me in pies
My father he ate me and said I was nice
My brothers and sisters they picked my bones
And they buried me under the marley stones.

*Derelict Woman muttering and shouting in the street. It is
the Skriker. Josie comes by.*

SKRIKER: I know my son is writing me letters all the
time and the army is stopping them because the officers are devils and do what you tell them because

they are DEVILS and the letters are in sacks in the
Bank of England waiting for the Day of Judgment
when you will go to HELL and lose sight of me and
stop moving me about but you can't move me now because my fingers are just so because I'm in charge of
the devils and if I keep it up the devils will let my son
go LET MY SON GO. What are you staring at?

JOSIE: You.

SKRIKER: Can you spare the price of a cup of / tea
darling

JOSIE: No.

SKRIKER: because I haven't eaten all day, bless you
for a sweet kind face. / I haven't eaten today but never

JOSIE: I said no.

SKRIKER: mind if you've no money my darling, that
happens to all of us, just give me a kiss instead. Won't
you give me / a kiss sweetheart?

JOSIE: Get off, you stinking crazy—

SKRIKER: You're a nasty girl, Josie, always were.

Skriker goes.

JOSIE: Is it you, come back, you—What? uh uh I'm
sick, what, it's alive, it's—it's toads is it, where from,
me is it, what?

*As she speaks toads come out of her mouth. She speaks
carefully, testing.*

When I speak, do toads—?

They do.

She opens her mouth to cry out in rage after Skriker, and shuts it, forcing herself to be silent to prevent more toads. She goes.

A Fair Fairy comes and tries to pick up the cake, the Man won't let her have it, she goes. He sits waiting. The Passerby is still dancing.

Josie and Lily are sitting on a sofa. Lily is wrapped in a blanket. The Skriker is part of the sofa, invisible to them.

During this, a Dark Fairy tries unsuccessfully to get the cake.

JOSIE: So you think it was just her got me out?

LILY: Because I wished it.

JOSIE: No I'm better, that's why.

LILY: And they bought you a train ticket?

JOSIE: They do that when they discharge you from hospital.

LILY: And how did you bump into me in the street?

JOSIE: Because I'm lucky.

Pause.

JOSIE: Aren't you glad to see me?

LILY: I don't feel very well. Is it cold in here?

JOSIE: No, it's fine.

LILY: I'm freezing.

JOSIE: You must be ill then.

LILY: Yes, I think I am.

JOSIE: Or that could be her.

Pause.

LILY: What could?

JOSIE: She's cold.

LILY: I'm cold because I'm ill, all right?

JOSIE: All right.

Pause.

JOSIE: Toads. She thinks she's funny. She's got it coming.

Pause.

LILY: Don't you think it's sad . . .

JOSIE: What?

Pause.

LILY: I think I'm fainting.

Pause. Lily touches Skriker.

Josie, there's something icy.

JOSIE: You better go to bed.

LILY: There's a thing. It's got a face.

JOSIE: Stop it.

LILY: Feel.

JOSIE: No.

LILY: I can see her. Josie, see her, you must.

JOSIE: She's for you now. You took her money.

LILY: No, I can't bear it, I wish / you'd—

JOSIE: Don't.

LILY: I wish you'd see her too.

Pause.

JOSIE: So I see her, so what?

SKRIKER: Josie's not frightened.

JOSIE: Toads, what you do that for, I'm not toads inside, it's you that's toads.

*Skriker leaps up out of the sofa. She's wearing a short pink
dress and gauzy wings.*

SKRIKER: Here I am as you can see
A fairy from a Christmas tree.
I can give you heart's desire
Help you set the world on fire.

LILY: This is a dream, it's a nightmare and I'll wake up.
I know I think other things happened like the money
but that's because I'm remembering it in the dream.

JOSIE: It's not a dream. She made me / speak toads.

LILY: You would say that because you're just somebody
in my dream.

JOSIE: I'm not, it's me, I'm awake.

SKRIKER: Don't you want a wish, Lily?

LILY: I'll tell you about it in the morning.

SKRIKER: What would you like, Lily?

JOSIE: Lily, / be careful.

LILY: I can't wake up yet but I can make it stop being a
nightmare.

JOSIE: Lily—

LILY: I wish for flowers.

*Flowers fall from above. Skriker takes Lily's hand and puts
it against her face.*

SKRIKER: I'm warmer now, feel.

LILY: And if it's not a dream it's even better.

The Green Lady comes for the cake. The Man gives it to her and she eats it. They go off together. The Passerby goes on dancing.

There is a row of small houses. The Spriggan and Raw-headandbloodybones tower over them.

A Black Dog.

Lily is in a park. A Small Child approaches her. It is the Skriker.

The Girl with the Telescope is looking through it but not seeing the Green Lady. She is tired and sad.

LILY: Can you play cat's cradle?

Skriker shakes her head.

   Shall I show you?

Skriker nods. Lily shows her cat's cradle.

   Put your fingers in here and take it. Good. Now I take it back. Now put your fingers, see, in there. Careful, that's it. Now I take it. Now you—that's right. This one's called fish in a dish. You use your little fingers and cross over—Oh it's all in a tangle.

SKRIKER: Do it again.

LILY: I'll show you one you can do by yourself.

Lily does it, Skriker watches. Josie comes and watches too.

LILY: There, do you like that?

SKRIKER: Show me again.

LILY: Watch what I'm doing. Get it like this to start. What's your name?

SKRIKER: I can do it. / Let me do it.

LILY: Wait. Where do you live?

SKRIKER: In the flats.

LILY: Have you got any brothers and sisters?

SKRIKER: Are you going to have a baby?

LILY: Yes.

SKRIKER: When?

LILY: Soon. There, do you like that?

Lily shows Skriker the cat's cradle.

SKRIKER: Can I be its sister?

LILY: You can't really be its sister.

SKRIKER: I can, I can be, please let me. I want a baby, I want a baby brother or a baby sister.

LILY: You'll have to ask your mum to have a baby.

SKRIKER: I haven't got a mum. Please let me be a sister. Say yes. Say yes. Please say yes.

LILY: Yes all right.

SKRIKER: I'll be its sister and you can be my mum.

LILY: Who do you live with?

SKRIKER: Please say yes. Pretend.

LILY: I'll be your pretend mum.

SKRIKER: Will you give me real dinner or pretend dinner?

LILY: Pretend dinner.

SKRIKER: Real sweets or pretend sweets?

LILY: I might find / some real sweets.

JOSIE: Do you like this child?

SKRIKER: Where? / Get some now. What kind?

LILY: Yes, I do.

JOSIE: She's horrible. There's something wrong with her.

Josie takes hold of Skriker to look at her.

LILY: Leave her alone.

SKRIKER: Leave me alone, I'll tell my mum.

JOSIE: She's not your mum. You haven't got a mum.

SKRIKER: Mum! mum!

LILY: Josie, stop it. It's all right, pet, she's just / teasing.

JOSIE: Get out you little scrounger. / Leave Lily alone.

SKRIKER: Mum, don't let her / hit me.

LILY: Josie.

JOSIE: I know you, you bastard. How you like toads? you like dirt in your mouth? Get away from us. You come in the house I'll put you in the fire, then we'll see what you look like.

Josie picks up dirt from the ground and stuffs it in the Skriker's mouth. Lily rescues Skriker.

LILY: Get away, you're crazy. / (*To Skriker.*) It's all

JOSIE: It's her.

SKRIKER: Mum, make her go away.

LILY: right. (*To Josie.*) I never want / to see you.

JOSIE: It's her.

LILY: Of course it's not her, it's a child, you're mad, you should have stayed in hospital, I can't look after you, you go round attacking people they'll take you away again and I won't care, I won't help you get out next time, / now go away and leave us alone.

JOSIE: She can have you then, I don't care, I'm not helping you.

Josie goes further away and watches.

LILY: Let's wipe your mouth. Poor baby. Did she hurt you? Nasty Josie.

SKRIKER: Nasty Josie. Nasty Josie. Nasty Josie.

LILY: Now where's our piece of string?

SKRIKER: Give me a cuddle. Let me sit on your lap.

LILY: Careful, mind my tummy.

SKRIKER: You're fat.

LILY: It's the baby.

SKRIKER: I'm the baby.

LILY: No, you're the baby's big sister.

SKRIKER: Fat fat fat.

LILY: Careful.

SKRIKER: Nasty baby.

She hits Lily's stomach.

LILY: Don't. Get off.

SKRIKER: Mum. Mum.

LILY: Come on then but be careful. Don't hurt the baby.

SKRIKER: Cuddle.

LILY: Cuddle cuddle.

SKRIKER: Kiss.

Lily kisses her.

LILY: Better now?

SKRIKER: Let's go home.

LILY: Home where?

SKRIKER: Where we live.

LILY: This is our house here.

SKRIKER: No I mean go home. To your house.

LILY: I better not take you back there. Someone's going to wonder where you are.

SKRIKER: No one's going to wonder. I want to go home. Take me home.

LILY: Let go, you're / pulling my hair.

SKRIKER: No no, hold me. Hold me.

LILY: Get down, / let go. Mind the baby.

SKRIKER: Hold me tight.

LILY: Let go. I'm telling you. / Now let go.

SKRIKER: Never never never / never.

LILY: You'll get a smack. Now get off. You're hurting. Get off.

She hits Skriker and pushes her away. Skriker lies on ground crying. Josie comes back.

Have I hurt her?

JOSIE: Not enough.

Skriker sits up.

SKRIKER: You touch me I'll tell my dad you'll be sorry, get my brother on you he's bigger than you, I got lots of friends / everywhere set them on you watch out get in your head get in your eyes turn you into dogshit on my shoe.

JOSIE: What you hurt me for, toads, what you do that for, I was looking for you, I'm not frightened, you're frightened, only did toads when I wasn't ready I'm ready now you just try you're no good there's something wrong with you you're a spastic fairy you need us more than we need you should have thought of that / before you done that to me too late.

LILY: Josie, it's not.

SKRIKER: You're stupid, aren't you, Lily. Josie knows.

JOSIE: Leave her alone, she can't—. You can come back to me.

SKRIKER: I don't want to. I like Lily.

JOSIE: But I wish it.

SKRIKER: I don't have to do what you wish. Lily doesn't wish it, do you?

LILY: I don't know.

SKRIKER: No because I might give you nice things. And Josie wants nice things. That's why she wants me. Not to help Lily. So you both want me. / That's nice.

LILY: I don't, no I don't.

SKRIKER: Josie's not frightened.

JOSIE: What do you want?

SKRIKER: I want a lot but so do you. We could both have it.

JOSIE: Have what?

SKRIKER: Whatever you like.

LILY: Josie, don't do it. When you feel her after you it's . . . Josie, remember what it felt like / before, don't do it.

JOSIE: But when you've lost her you want her back. Because you see what she can do and you've lost your chance and it could be the only chance ever / in my life to—

LILY: Josie, don't.

SKRIKER: I knew you were desperate, that's how I
   found you. Are you ready now?

LILY: Josie, I wish / you wouldn't.

SKRIKER: You don't count any more.

Pause.

JOSIE: Yes.

*Blackout. A horrible shriek like a siren that goes up to a
very high sound and holds it. Gradually it relents little by
little breaking up into notes and coming down till it is
pleasant and even melodious.*

*Underworld. As Skriker and Josie arrive it springs into
existence. Light, music, long table with feast, lavishly
dressed people and creature, such as Yallery Brown, Nellie
Longarms, Jenny Greenteeth, the Kelpie, Black Dog,
Rawheadandbloodybones, the Radiant Boy, Johnny
Squarefoot, Black Annis (with a blue face and one eye). It
looks wonderful except that it is all glamour and here and
there it's not working—some of the food is twigs, leaves,
beetles, some of the clothes are rags, some of the beautiful
people have a claw hand or hideous face. But the first
impression is of a palace. Skriker is a fairy queen, dressed
grandiosely, with lapses.*

*As they arrive the rest burst into song. Everyone except
Josie and the Skriker sings instead of speaking. They press
food and drink on Josie, greet her, touch her.*

SPIRITS: Welcome homesick
   drink drank drunk
   avocado and prawn cockfight cockup cocksuck

red wine or white wash
champagne the pain is a sham pain the pain is a
   sham
fillet steak fill it up stakes in your heart
meringue utang
black coffee fi fo fum.

A Hag rushes in shrieking. She seizes food, scattering it, searching. She sings.

HAG: Where's my head? where's my heart? where's my arm? where's my leg? is that my finger? that's my eye.

The Spirits laugh and jeer at her and repeat what she says, singing.

SPIRITS: Headlong . . . heartthrob . . . harmful
. . . legless . . . finicky . . . eyesore.

HAG: Give me my bones.

Josie and Skriker speak, everyone else sings.

JOSIE: What is it? what's the matter?

HAG: They cut me up. They boiled me for dinner. Where's my head? is that my shoulder? that's my toe.

SKRIKER: They chopped her to pieces, they chipped her to pasties. She's a hag higgledepig hog. She's a my my miser myselfish and chips.

SPIRITS: A miser a miserable

HAG: Give me my bones.

The Spirits jeer and pelt the Hag with bits of food and drive her away.

They repeat previous singing about the feast. A lost girl takes Josie aside and sings to her under cover of the other singing.

GIRL: Don't eat. It's glamour. It's twigs and beetles and a dead body. Don't eat or you'll never get back.

The Spirits urge food on Josie and the Girl has to move away. But she manages to get back.

Don't drink. It's glamour. It's blood and dirty water. I was looking for my love and I got lost in an orchard. Never take an apple, never pick a flower. I took one bite and now I'm here forever. Everyone I love must be dead by now. Don't eat, don't drink, or you'll never get back.

Spirits push her aside and sing on, louder and more chaotically. Skriker offers Josie a glass of red wine.

SKRIKER: Your wealth, Josie, happy and gory.

JOSIE: I'm not thirsty.

SKRIKER: Thirst and worst, mouth drouth dry as dustbowl.

JOSIE: Yes, but I don't—

SKRIKER: Dizzy dozy chilly shally.

JOSIE: Yes but I don't want—

SKRIKER: Don't you want to feel global warm and happy ever after? Warm the cackles of your heartless. Make you brave and rave. Look at the colourful, smell the tasty. Won't you drink a toasty with me, Josie, after all we've done for?

Josie drinks. Everyone is silent and attentive for a moment. Then they all burst out singing again triumphantly, among them The Girl sings.

GIRL: Twigs and beetles and dead body. Water and blood. You'll never get back.

But Josie doesn't notice her. She is happy now and eats the food they pile in front of her, not noticing the difference between cake and twigs. The Spirits celebrate, congratulating the Skriker.

SPIRITS: We won wonderful
    full up at last
    last man's dead.

One by one the spirits get up and dance, and Josie and the Skriker too, increasing frenzy. Some of them fly into the air.

In the confusion the feast disintegrates. Finally everything and everyone has gone except the Passerby still dancing.

Silence and gloom. Josie appears on her hands and knees scrubbing the floor. A Monster comes to watch her. It is the Skriker. There is a fountain.

SKRIKER: Better butter bit of better bitter but you're better off down here you arse over tit for tattle, arsy versy, verse or prose or amateur status the nation wide open wide world hurled hurtling hurting hurt very badly. Wars whores hips hip hoorays it to the ground glass. Drought rout out and about turn off. Sunburn sunbeam in your eye socket to him. All good many come to the aids party. When I go uppety, follow a fellow on a dark road dank ride and jump thrump out and eat him how does he taste? toxic waste paper basket case, salmonelephantiasis, blue blood bad blood blue blood blad blood blah blah blah. I remember dismember the sweet flesh in the panic, tearing limb from lamb chop you up and suck the tomorrow bones. Lovely lively lads and maiden England, succulent suck your living daylights, sweet blood like seawater everywhere, every bite did you good enough as good as a feast.

JOSIE: And now no one tastes any good?

SKRIKER: Dry as dustpans, foul as shitpandemonium. Poison in the food chain saw massacre.

JOSIE: If I could just go and see. I'd come back.

SKRIKER: Shall I take you in my pocket pick it up and tuck it in?

JOSIE: Yes please.

SKRIKER: Up in the smokey hokey pokey? up in the world wind? up in the war zone ozone zany grey?

JOSIE: Because it's years. I think I've lived longer than they do up there. If I don't go now I won't know anyone.

SKRIKER: What will you pay me say the bells the bells?

JOSIE: Sip my blood?

SKRIKER: Haven't I sipped lipped lapped your pretty twist wrist for years and fears? What's happy new, what's special brew hoo?

JOSIE: I had a dream last night.

SKRIKER: Haven't I wrapped myself up rapt rapture ruptured myself in your dreams, scoffed your chocolate screams, your Jung men and Freud eggs, your flying and fleeing? It was golden olden robes you could rip tide me up in but now it's a tatty bitty scarf scoff scuffle round my nickneck. Give a dog a bone.

JOSIE: Tell you something I remember.

SKRIKER: Haven't I drained rained sprained ankles and uncles, aunts and answers, father and nearer? What do you know about your selfish you haven't worn down out?

JOSIE: Got a new one.

SKRIKER: Bran tub new? lucky dipstick?

JOSIE: Never even thought it myself. Something I saw when I was three.

SKRIKER: What?

JOSIE: Will you take me up?

SKRIKER: What?

JOSIE: A little bit of stony ground.

SKRIKER: And?

JOSIE: It had little stones on it.

SKRIKER: Were you alonely?

JOSIE: I don't remember. Probably alone. No, probably someone nearby. I remember the stones.

SKRIKER: What can I do with a scrap crap wrap myself up in it? Ground to a halt. Stone death.

JOSIE: But you'll take me with you?

SKRIKER: That doesn't bye bye a trip up. You're dry as dead leaves you behind.

JOSIE: Please.

SKRIKER: You'll never go home on the range rover's return again witless.

JOSIE: Why not, if I'm useless?

SKRIKER: When I'm weak at the need, you'll be a last tiny totter of whisky whistle to keep my spirits to keep me stronger linger longer gaga. And while I'm await a minute, don't touch the water baby.

JOSIE: Don't touch the water in the fountain because I'll die.

Skriker goes.

Josie goes to the fountain and almost puts her hand in the water.

She shrieks and plunges her hands in. A shrieking sound gets louder and louder.

Darkness.

Johnny Squarefoot throwing stones at Black Dog.

Josie, Lily and the Skriker as child are exactly as they were in the park. Skriker runs off.

The Black Dog is in the park. The Girl with the Telescope sits depressed. The Kelpie and the Woman who rode off on his back stroll as lovers.

LILY (*shouting after Skriker*):   We're not scared of you.

   (*To Josie.*) It's just a child anyway.

JOSIE: Too bright. My eyes don't work. Hold me.

LILY: Now what?

JOSIE: You smell like people. Your hair's like hair. It was like putting a gun to my head because they always said I'd die if I did that. Liars, you hear me? I got away. Yah. Can't get me.

LILY: Stop it. You can stop it.

JOSIE: I was ready to die. I thought I'd never get back.

LILY: Don't. It makes me lonely.

JOSIE: That's right I'm not dead? We're not both dead? Lily, you didn't die while I was away?

LILY: Josie.

JOSIE: No, tell me are we dead?

LILY: No we're not. Stop it.

JOSIE: How long's it been?

LILY: How long's what?

JOSIE: I went for.

LILY: Come on, let's go home.

JOSIE: I had a whole life. How long? I'm very old.

LILY: You went? what?

JOSIE: Years and years, longer than I lived here, I wasn't much more than a child here hardly. I've got children there, Lily, and they're grown up but I didn't mean to leave them, I thought I'd just die, won't I ever see them? I don't want to go back. How can I live now?

LILY: You can't be old. Look at you. Look at me.

JOSIE: Yes, how do you do that? You've travelled into the future. You're not real. You're something she's made up.

LILY: Josie. (*Lily hugs her.*)

JOSIE: Are you glad to see me?

LILY: I never stopped seeing you.

JOSIE: But you're glad?

LILY: Yes.

JOSIE: When is this? I don't know when it is.

LILY: It's just today like it's been all day. We went to the shops. We met a child in the park.

JOSIE: That's horrible.

LILY: Please, I'm tired. My stomach hurts.

JOSIE: No time at all?

As they go the Bucket and Cloth Man and the Green Lady go by. He is weak and stumbling. The Black Dog follows them off. The Depressed Girl goes on sitting.

A Businessman with a Thrumpin riding on his back. He doesn't know it's there. The Girl leaves. He is joined by colleagues, all with Thrumpins, for a meeting. They are talking but we can't hear what they say. All we can hear is a shrill twittering wordless conversation among the Thrumpins. Still Passerby dancing.

A smart Woman in mid thirties. It is the Skriker.

SKRIKER: So the Skriker sought fame and fortune telling, celebrity knockout drops, TV stardomination, chat showdown and market farces, see if I carefree, and completely forgetmenot Lily and Josie. Lovely and

Juicy, silly and cosy, lived in peaces and quite, Jerky
still mad as a hitter and Lively soon gave happy birth to
a baby a booby a babbly byebye booboo boohoo
hoooooo. What a blossom bless 'em. Dear little mighty.

Lily and Josie and the baby are on the sofa. Rawheadand-
bloodybones sits on a shelf watching, invisible to them.
Skriker and Men with Thrumpins leave.

LILY: Everyone says you'll be tired or they . . . bun-
nies or fluffy . . . everything too sweet and you think
that's really boring, makes you want to dress her in
black but she's not sweet like pink and blue. Or you get
them moaning about never get enough sleep or oh my
stitches or like that, no one lets on.

JOSIE: Are you listening to me?

LILY: Day and night.

JOSIE: But in fact never.

LILY: I'm tired.

JOSIE: You just said tired wasn't it.

LILY: It's not all about it but I'm still tired.

JOSIE: So what's the big secret?

LILY: Not a secret.

JOSIE: What's so wonderful wonderful only you're bril-
liant enough to feel it?

LILY: Nothing.

JOSIE: Everyone gets born you know. It's not something you invented. Walk down the street you'll see several people that were born.

Silence.

LILY: So tell me again.

Silence.

Josie, it's over.

JOSIE: How can it be over if it didn't happen?

LILY: What you thought what you dreamed whatever is over.

JOSIE: But I did go.

LILY: Josie, I was with you all the time.

JOSIE: But I did go.

LILY: All right.

JOSIE: Smash your face in. I did go. They need us you know, they think we're magic. They drink your blood. I miss the dancing.

Silence.

JOSIE: So what is it about her?

LILY: I know everyone's born. I can't help it. Everything's shifted round so she's in the middle. I never minded things. But everything dangerous seems it

might get her. I know she's just . . . But if she wasn't
all right it'd be a waste, wouldn't it.

JOSIE: What happened to me is like that. As big as that
is to you. I promise.

LILY: But it happened in no time at all.

JOSIE: Yes. But where I was it was years.

LILY: Yes.

JOSIE: All right then.

LILY: And it's over now.

JOSIE: Everything's flat here like a video. There's
something watching us.

LILY: Yes but there's not.

JOSIE: I can't go back because they hate me for getting
away.

LILY: You want to go back?

JOSIE: I'm never going to be all right.

LILY: You know how they say 'oh their little fingers'
and of course they've got little fingers, they couldn't
have fingers like us. But that's not what they mean. I
mean look at her fingers.

JOSIE: She's a changeling.

LILY: She what?

JOSIE: That's not your baby. They've put one of theirs and taken yours off.

LILY: Don't say that, don't.

JOSIE: Changeling. / Changeling.

LILY: I warn you, I'll kill you / don't say it.

JOSIE: You believe me don't you?

LILY: I don't want, I don't believe you no / but I

JOSIE: Lucky for them.

LILY: don't want to hear it.

JOSIE: They'll keep yours down there. It makes them stronger. They'll breed from it. And you'll always have this one watching you. Look at its little slitty eye.

LILY: Don't even think it. / I'm not listening.

JOSIE: Shall I tell you what? if you want your own one back? You put the changeling on a shovel and put it in the fire, that's what they used to do. So we'd use the cooker and put it over the gas. And sometimes they turn into a cat and go up the chimney. How'd it get out of here? Round and round the walls. I'll open the window. Then you get your own one back in the cot.

LILY: I can't live with you if you're like this.

JOSIE: You've got to fight them. You say you love her and you won't even do something to get her back. This isn't human. I can tell.

LILY: Whatever you are, if you're really there, if you can hear me, I want a wish.

JOSIE: She'll come back, look out.

LILY: I wish Josie wasn't mad.

JOSIE: Don't wish me.

Silence.

LILY: Did anything happen?

JOSIE: What have you done?

LILY: What have I done?

JOSIE: Hurts.

LILY: Where? what?

JOSIE: Inside.

LILY: What have they done to you?

JOSIE: Here.

LILY: I wish—

JOSIE: Don't don't don't.

LILY: What have they done?

JOSIE: I don't think anything's broken. They haven't really put bits of metal. I killed her. Did I? Yes. I hadn't forgotten but. She was just as precious. Yours isn't the only. If I hadn't she'd still. I keep knowing it again, what can I do? Why did I? It should have been me. Because under that pain oh shit there's under that under that there's this other / under that there's—

LILY: Wait, stop, I'm sorry, I'll / fix it

JOSIE: Don't let me feel it. It's coming for me. Hide me. This is what. When I killed her. What I was frightened. Trying to stop when I. It's here.

LILY: No please I'll—

JOSIE: Save me. Can you? There's no one to save.

LILY: I wish—

JOSIE: No.

LILY: If I wish you happy, no, you could kill people and still, don't feel pain no, just all right what does that mean, I wish I hadn't, no I'd do it again, I wish you were like before I wished, does that, I wish—

JOSIE: You mustn't keep wishing or she'll get you.

LILY: Are you all right now?

JOSIE: There's something.

LILY: What?

JOSIE: Gone.

LILY: It doesn't hurt?

JOSIE: What? (*Silence.*)

LILY: I should have asked you.

JOSIE: Well ask me.

LILY: If you really thought . . .

JOSIE: Are you starting again? I was there for years.

LILY: No, if you thought she was a changeling.

JOSIE: Shall we do some tests? Yeah? Be a laugh.

LILY: No we won't. We'll take care of her.

JOSIE: Have you been wishing? Stupid. She'll get you now.

Many couples dancing. They include Kelpie and Woman, Green Lady and Bucket Man, who is weak, Brownie, Skriker as man, Rawheadandbloodybones, Black Dog, Johnny Squarefoot, Nellie Longarms. There is a large shoe and when they've finished dancing they climb on it. It is identical to Lily's shoe which she has kicked off. She is sitting on the sofa with a Man about 30. It is the Skriker. Josie is chopping vegetables. The Baby is in a carrycot.

SKRIKER: I'd wait down the end of the road and see you come out with the pram. I'd watch you in the park.

LILY: When did you?

SKRIKER: You knew I was there though.

LILY: No, when?

SKRIKER: You meant me to follow you or I wouldn't
  have done it.

LILY: I never saw you.

SKRIKER: Unconsciously meant. Or in your stars.
  Some deep . . .

LILY: Oh like that.

SKRIKER: Yes some fateful . . . So that when we met
  it wasn't for the first time. You felt that. Some people
  are meant to be together. I'd walk out of meetings because of this overpowering . . . I'd accelerate to fifty
  on a short block up to a red light. Anything that wasn't
  you my eyes veered off. I couldn't sleep, of course, not
  that sleep's my best—do you sleep?

LILY: If she lets me.

SKRIKER: How do you do that? No what do you do,
  tell me. You go to bed.

LILY: I go to bed.

SKRIKER: You take anything?

LILY: Not to sleep, no, be a waste.

SKRIKER: So you just lie down.

LILY: I might look at a magazine for about ten minutes
  but then I'm too sleepy.

SKRIKER: So what's that like when you get sleepy?

LILY: You know what it's like.

SKRIKER: No, what's it like.

Josie goes out.

LILY: My eyes keep shutting by themselves. I'm reading something and then I see my eyes are shut so I
open them and think I'll just finish that story and the
words are going double so I don't bother. So I put out
the light.

SKRIKER: And then what?

LILY: I go to sleep.

SKRIKER: No, how? What happens.

LILY: I'm lying there. And . . .

SKRIKER: And thoughts.

LILY: Maybe thoughts a bit about the day or—

SKRIKER: Rush through your head.

LILY: Not rush but . . . and I might see things.

SKRIKER: See . . . ?

LILY: Like a tree with its leaves or somebody . . .

SKRIKER: Frightening things?

LILY: No but nothing to do with anything, not dreams
exactly but bright—and I know something I've just

thought isn't right, like maybe there's two things that seem to be something to do with each other but they're not but I can't remember what it was—

SKRIKER: Your mind's going out of control like when there's going to be an accident. / When any

LILY: No.

SKRIKER: minute people are going to be mangled in some machinery and it's going very slowly but you can't / stop it.

LILY: No, not like that.

SKRIKER: Like what?

LILY: Nothing, I'm asleep after that.

SKRIKER: So maybe that's something I'd pick up. I'd slide off into sleep beside you.

LILY: Why don't you sleep?

SKRIKER: I have slept. It's partly my legs, they can't get right. And things in my head. Well I'll tell you there was this . . . He was quite highpowered, he thought he was. He was going to help me, he was going to manage me because I was a conjuror at this point, I could do these amazing—I was entitled to recognition. He didn't deliver. So I'd lie awake. Well he subsequently died in fact. So that was good. But I've got a lot on my mind. You'll help me with that.

LILY: I don't know.

SKRIKER: Yes because you have faith in me.

Josie comes back.

Have you noticed the large number of meteorological phenomena lately? Earthquakes. Volcanoes. Drought. Apocalyptic meteorological phenomena. The increase of sickness. It was always possible to think whatever your personal problem, there's always nature. Spring will return even if it's without me. Nobody loves me but at least it's a sunny day. This has been a comfort to people as long as they've existed. But it's not available any more. Sorry. Nobody loves me and the sun's going to kill me. Spring will return and nothing will grow. Some people might feel concerned about that. But it makes me feel important. I'm going to be around when the world as we know it ends. I'm going to witness unprecedented catastrophe. I like a pileup on the motorway. I like the kind of war we're having lately. I like snuff movies. But this is going to be the big one.

Josie goes out.

Your friend doesn't like me.

LILY: I'm sorry.

SKRIKER: I'm getting uncomfortable.

LILY: She doesn't like anyone.

SKRIKER: I can't tolerate being disliked. So never mind. We'll go away together. You'd like a holiday. We'll bring the baby, no problem, I love kids, babies are cupid. What are you doing tomorrow?

LILY: No, I—

SKRIKER: You think this is sudden. I think it's sudden. No I don't. I've been looking for you. It's going to happen.

LILY: What's going to happen?

SKRIKER: Us being together forever. We both know that. So there's no point taking a long time getting to the point which we got to the first time no even before we met no even before I ever set eyes on you because this kind of thing is meant. Don't you agree?

LILY: Yes I do. I think I do.

SKRIKER: What's this 'I think'?

LILY: I just . . .

SKRIKER: Are you backing out?

LILY: No. What? I—

SKRIKER: Don't do this to me. I warn you. Quite straightforwardly as one human being to another.

LILY: I didn't mean—

SKRIKER: Don't don't don't don't don't look startled. You're the only good person I've ever met. Everyone else has tried to destroy me. But you wish me well. You wouldn't deny that.

LILY: No, I—

SKRIKER: No.

LILY: No I—

SKRIKER: What? what? don't dare. This is a high volt-
age cable. Are you going to grab it? I'm going to take
care of you and the baby. You're coming with me. You
don't have to worry about anything any more.

Josie comes in again.

LILY: I do like you. I can't look away from you. But a
bit slower. It's no use getting angry because I can't—

SKRIKER: I hate it when I'm so unkind. This sometimes happens. I won't go into my childhood just now.
I can't forgive myself. I feel terrible.

LILY: I didn't mean—

SKRIKER: I'm useless, I get something beautiful and I
ruin it. Everything I touch falls apart. There are some
people who deserve to be killed and I believe it's important to be completely without remorse. I admire
that if someone has no compassion because that's what
it takes. But other people such as yourself. You won't
want to see me again. How could I do that? I worship
you. I'm so ashamed. I feel sick. Help me. Forgive me.
Could you ever love me?

*Josie attacks him with a knife, slashing his arm and chest.
Blood on his shirt.*

Do you love me? Do you love me?

LILY: Yes, yes I do.

He takes off the bloodstained shirt and tie. Underneath, identical clean ones.

SKRIKER (*to Josie*):   You're getting into a lot of trouble. She loves me.

LILY: No I don't. What are you?

SKRIKER: But you do you know. See you later.

He goes.

LILY: These things only come because of you. Go and live somewhere else.

Green Lady pushing Bucket Man in a wheelchair.

Kelpie with the body of Woman who went away with him.

Telescope Girl distraught and searching. Josie leaves with Black Dog.

Passerby still dancing.

Marie, a young woman about Lily's age, is visiting Lily. It is the Skriker. The Kelpie cuts up the woman's body.

SKRIKER: Can I pick up the baby?

LILY: No.

SKRIKER: Sorry.

LILY: I don't remember you.

SKRIKER: I've grown up.

Silence.

Someone's going to kill me. Marie never hung out with the right people. I need somewhere to stay.

LILY: I can't help you.

SKRIKER: You're not the only person I know. I'm almost a celebrity. My face has been on the covers—not this face exactly but a face. But I'm the same old Marie. Those are silver, these are gold. There's a lot of people out there who pretend to be your friend. They say they are. But you and me and Josie swore in blood.

LILY: I don't remember.

SKRIKER: You remember the waste ground? you remember the corner with the nettles? you remember Josie?

LILY: Of course I remember Josie.

SKRIKER: You've forgotten Marie.

LILY: I'm sorry . . . I can't . . . I'm not sure.

SKRIKER: When we left messages in the wall?

LILY: Yes I do remember the wall.

SKRIKER: The tree.

LILY: Corner shop after school.

SKRIKER: Sherbet lemons.

LILY: But were you . . . ?

SKRIKER: It's funny how much of our life we forget. You can't help it. You never liked me best. Let me stay with you. There's room now Josie's gone. I'd be safe here.

LILY: No.

SKRIKER: My dad did things to me. I never told you that. My mum shut me in the cupboard.

LILY: Go somewhere else.

SKRIKER: My boyfriend's going to kill me.

LILY: You're not Marie.

SKRIKER: No, but I'm still in danger. That's why I came. Look, I'm not pretending anything. That's good isn't it? You've got to love me.

LILY: How would that help?

SKRIKER: Yes, help me Lily. I don't work properly. You've got to come with me. You can save me. You want to.

LILY: I don't love you at all. I don't like you. I don't care if you die. I'm never going to see you again.

Skriker goes. Lily sits exhausted. Later she goes.

A Family having a picnic on a beach. The beach is covered with Blue Men. Passerby still dancing.

Josie and the Black Dog are in a small room, visited by a shabby respectable Man about 40. It is the Skriker.

JOSIE: She didn't know anyone. She didn't have anywhere to stay the night. I slipped a wire loop over her head.

Skriker laughs.

So that'll do for a bit, yeh? You'll feel ok. There's an earthquake on the telly last night. There's a motorway pileup in the fog.

SKRIKER: You're a good girl, Josie.

JOSIE: There's dead children.

SKRIKER: Tell me more about her.

JOSIE: She had red hair. She had big feet. She liked biscuits. She woke up while I was doing it. But you didn't do the carcrash. You'd tell me. You're not strong enough to do an earthquake.

Skriker coughs.

I'll do terrible things, I promise. Just leave it to me. You don't have to do anything. Don't do anything. Promise.

Skriker coughs.

You won't do anything to Lily?

SKRIKER: Who's Lily?

JOSIE: Nobody. Someone you used to know. You've forgotten her.

Skriker laughs.

Have you forgotten her?

Skriker coughs.

I think you'd like me to do something tomorrow.

Skriker coughs.

The Bucket Man comes slowly in his wheelchair, moving it himself now. He stops and dozes. The Telescope Girl comes in, she has bandaged wrists. Rawheadand-bloodybones, Kelpie and Johnny Squarefoot rush across wildly, tangling with the Passerby, who keeps dancing.

SKRIKER: Josie went further and murther in the dark, trying to keep the Skriker sated seated besotted with gobbets, tossing it giblets, to stop it from wolfing, stop it engulfing. But still there was gobbling and gabbling, giggling and gaggling, biting and beating, eating and hating, hooting and looting and lightning and thunder in the southeast northwest northeast southwest north-south crisis. Lily doolalley was living in peacetime, no more friend, no more fiend, safe as dollshouses. But she worried and sorried and lay far awake into the night-mare. Poor furry, she thought, pure feary, where are you now and then? And something drove her over and over and out of her mind how you go.

Black Annis has small houses in a glass aquarium. She slowly fills it with water.

Lily, with the Baby, arrives at the hospital, where there is a very ill old woman. It is the Skriker.

LILY: What you doing in hospital? If you're really asleep I'll say it again after. I thought you'd be in the government or the movies by now. I went to stations when people were coming off trains or closing time coming out of pubs. I'd put her in the pram, she'd go back to sleep. There are things out in the night. I think you should be glad I've come, and open your eyes. When I made you go I didn't know you'd really gone, anyone spoke to me I was frightened. Then one day there was someone going to jump from a building and when it wasn't you I started looking.

SKRIKER: Don't kill me.

LILY: It's Lily.

SKRIKER: They've taken my friends away. Not me.

LILY: I'll take care of you.

SKRIKER: You're a liar, Lily.

LILY: I came to find you.

SKRIKER: I had a friend fed her cat on tins and it was frightened of real food. Put a bit of raw meat down and it lept back. It smelt blood. Thought it was going to eat it. The dinner the cat. I've enemies in here. Shh.

LILY: I came to say I'd go with you.

SKRIKER: Where are you going, dear?

LILY: You said you wanted me to. Like Josie.

SKRIKER: I've no idea who these people are.

LILY: Yes because I miss . . . You'll leave everyone else alone if I do that, I'm not bringing the baby so don't ask, you're to leave her alone always. And Josie alone. Because if I go it'll help, won't it?

SKRIKER: Have you tried dialling 999?

LILY: I know I said I didn't love you.

SKRIKER: Aren't you afraid a fade away?

LILY: No because if it's what Josie did I'll be back in no time. It could feel like hundreds of years and I wouldn't leave the baby for five minutes but when I get back she won't know I've gone.

SKRIKER: Gone with the wind hover crafty.

LILY: Even if it's a nightmare. I'll be back the same second. I'll make you safe. Take me with you.

Skriker leaps up. It is no longer the old woman. It is the Skriker from the beginning of the piece, but full of energy.

SKRIKER: Lily, my heartthrobber baron, my solo flighty, now I've some blood in my all in veins, now I've some light in my lifeline nightline nightlight a candle to light you to bedlam, here comes a—

Skriker lights a candle and gives it to Lily

Watch the lightyear. Here you stand in an enchanted

wood you or wouldn't you. Just hold this candle the scandal I said and she stood till stood still stood till what?

Lily stands holding the candle. Everything else is dark. A blackbird sings.

An Old Woman and a Deformed Girl sitting together. They see Lily appear. The Girl cries out. The candle goes out and Lily sees them.

The Passerby is still dancing.

Lily appeared like a ghastly, made their hair stand on endless night, their blood run fast. 'Am I in fairy-landed?' she wandered. 'No,' said the old crony, 'this is the real world' whirl whir wh wh what is this? Lily was solid flash. If she was back on earth where on earth where was the rockabye baby gone the treetop? Lost and gone for everybody was dead years and tears ago, it was another cemetery, a black whole hundred yearns. Grief struck by lightning. And this old dear me was Lily's granddaughter what a horror storybook ending. 'Oh I was tricked tracked wracked,' cried our heroine distress, 'I hoped to save the worldly, I hoped I'd make the fury better than she should be.' And what would be comfy of her now? She didn't know if she ate a mortal morsel she'd crumble to dust panic. Are you my grand great grand great are you my child's child's child's? But when the daughters grand and great greater greatest knew she was from the distant past master class, then rage raging bullfight bullroar.

The Girl bellows wordless rage at Lily.

'Oh they couldn't helpless,' said the granddaughter,

'they were stupid stupefied stewpotbellied not evil weevil devil take the hindmost of them anyway.' But the child hated the monstrous.

Girl bellows.

'Leave her alone poor little soul-o,' said the grin dafter, 'cold in the headache, shaking and shocking. Have a what drink, wrap her in a blanket out, have a sandwhich one would you like?' So Lily bit off more than she could choose. And she was dustbin.

The Old Woman holds out some food and Lily puts out her hand to take it.

The Passerby stops dancing.

End.